The Complete Works of Mattie McClane

Volume Two, Poetry

MYRTLE HEDGE PRESS

Copyright © 2026 by Myrtle Hedge Press, Kure Beach NC
All rights reserved
Printed in the United States of America

ISBN: 978-1-7329970-7-3
Library of Congress Control Number:

Design and layout by Val Sherer, Personalized Publishing Services

No part of this book may be used, reproduced, or transmitted in any form or by any means, electronic or mechanical, including photocopying, recording or by any information storage and retrieval system, without written permission from the author, except in the case of brief quotations embodied in critical articles and reviews.

Contents

Now Time 1

Stations of the Cross 129

The Mother Word 171

The Song of the Grackle 203

The Magnificent Light of Morning . . . 237

To Free the Sisters of Mary 269

At the Edge of the Cities Burning . . . 291

The Tale of the Ancient Haberdasher . . 311

Occupying Nazareth 331

About the Author 349

Now Time

Now Time

The clouds build
toward the lilies;
the sky is faintly purple
with rain. These words lend hope
or a consolation from being away.
The trees are still as if they are listening
to mild rumblings; thunder
begins in the distance and comes closer to home.
One wonders what happens now, the old computer
was so hacked. so undone, that another
replaces it. My soul, my soul longs for beauty
and to be concise in all things.

I think of things unresolved, of loose ends
and unfinished questions. Of course, when
we are young we believe that we can walk
away from turmoil. But it finds us like work,
like the carpet that needs sweeping
or the grass that grows long. It has found me.
And I do long for the pleasant past when
worries were passed over. I do long for when
I was able to express deepest thoughts without

anxiety. I think I've been wrong for sounding
so right, for saying what nobody can know
for sure. Be wary of quick inspiration and easy-flowing words.
Words come hard when they are yours. I say we push
on moisture-swollen doors, an immovable thought;
but I can break through and the words will look like
they belong in rich hotels with foil wrapped candy
on pillows. They'll be as sweet as wedding icing
or summer clover. You pick. I can pick through
words until the exhausted verb falls on the page, a swoon
like movie lovers with thick lips and strange names.
Only I will find it hard to be fake; I will find it
difficult to frame silly ideas in the noblest terms. Go figure,
a model's shape, rectangles, squares and oblong boobs.
I am the fool today because I thought I could know
truth and it ran out the opened gate or under, yes under
the fence when I wasn't looking or was reading
the New York Times, the only newspaper that can use
the word, sublime, how excellent, how perfect, just elevated
like a spike heel, I will want to be healed
because I didn't really know a damned thing
with my multiple degrees.

A person should have one degree, preferably in chemistry
and know the facts, measurements, atomic numbers, even
naturally occurring elements. Leave it to no one to judge,

to surmise motives; it'll turn one
into a toady and then what?
One will carry a footstool with a satin covering messed up
with boot black. Remember the accusation that one didn't
know shit from shoe shine? That's how it happens, any toady
might tell me. Let's move on though… Words won't slide
on a page; they're not zealous baseball players or skaters.
I tell you they resist and would laugh at me maybe if they
could tell what I'm trying to do.

Newspapers are full of words, and they go out everyday. They
can't hang around saying the same thing like books. Who can
throw out a book?
Probably a sinister man or an anal woman
who keeps her magazines
on a coffee table. Books are for keeps. That is the unspoken
vow and it is real, all those words on parade, floats at a county
fair celebration,
one after another, but nobody throws candy and nobody
waves from convertibles. Books are stately, no Nebraska
irrigation machine ever
looked so fine, a lofty and noticeable presence.

Words aren't easy and books do not go to recyclers,
they offer no choices of plastic;
it's paper all the way. Someone said it was an apple

that caused the problem
but it was paper.

It's hot today-h-o-t-t, as the man at the farmer's market says. He sold me a
paper sack of grass seed. Seed is as pretty as oats. I threw the seed with a hand-
spreader and dogs trampled any beginnings. They did not know it was
for the lawn. It was a tickertape parade or a confetti extravaganza. The dogs
thought a war was over.

Unresolved matters are everywhere, the war in Iraq. Nobody
knows why we're there, oil, freedom, we're the liberators
of people
who didn't want to be free, we're unwanted helping hands,
setting up democracy in a tradition of tyranny. Tyrants
wear mustaches
and the media reports on their snacking habits, no
potato chips
for a menace. The media doesn't report harsh words
about America,
because they are the bad guys. We are good, have usually
been good in history.

I turned on the porch light last night,
wanted everyone to know
that there's a house in the woods. The bugs swooned around
the light; light is tequila to them; they are intoxicated
by the light.
No deliveryman came, no UPS, no Fed Ex,
no courier of any kind,
so someone flipped the switch, and it was trees in darkness,
trees
see nothing, and they don't use words.
Trees are poems, aren't pretenders
or rhetoricians. They could care less about the political
implications
in narratives.

Pink myrtle blooms in September, late
like news about a job
when one wants to work
at a desk, a sturdy table
to spread out papers
meant for file cabinets
ancient orange, painted
for home offices, and the buds
have yellow seeds, we're back
to seeds that make everything grow
and prosper; it is a prosperous era,

a deep-pocket time, jingle coins silver
but there is no gold in plastic
just a monthly statement
when the myrtles bloom late
like expecting a baby; one
go to the doctor and say
the water has broken, water, drip,
up to ceilings in places after
a record number of hurricanes,
who will say to generations
that Chicago is the Windy City,
New Orleans knows better
under the events center thousands
take shelter.

The disaster was worse than expected
with hundreds missing, hundreds dead.
Rehnquist dies and now the battle
is for the Supreme Court
and the catastrophe is nearly forgotten
to politics. "Today" is the strongest word
there isn't another like it with so much agency,
so much urgency, and promises kept.
If I can do it today, I'm a healer,
a triumph, a success story, the world marvels
at heroism. Where are the heroes? Did they die

in the early to mid 20th century? Are they
gone? The air is clear
as if it were a sandwich bag;
it is clear and keeps fresh, pears hanging
from a bowed-over tree
with a hundred limbs aimed
toward the ground, dusty ground,
and one looks for rain
but the forecaster says sunny
more dryness, more uncertainty.
Yet, perhaps hope is in the falling mercury,
down it goes for the ninth month, changing green
to multi-colored horizons,
one tires of the monotony of illness
to too much heat, too much stillness,
and longs for newness.
What is new in your bag of tricks?
What thing, gizmo or gadget can win
the popular sentiment
like the dream of affectionate strangers
with kin-like hugs and well-wishes
and longtime curious readers call
or write in wanting
to know where I've been, away
on vacation, always away on vacation
when a call comes from Ohio;

the lady phones from a white barn
with oat bins and calves,
an advertisement painted
on the sliding shed door
so it can be seen from the interstate
by tourists or people going home
to somewhere, a white farmhouse surrounded
by churches and noticeable steeples,
held high from the summer's turning wind
and Dorothy runs for the cellar this time
and no one makes a movie
about her adventures, no one should tell
that story again for another year,
the children do not gather
like they used to in front
of the television and stay up late
to know the fate of the man behind
the curtain; the call will come
in from Eastern Kentucky
and the incoming voice will offer
me everything, every kind of work,
every type of class, and amazement
has her day and will be female
for the purpose of this poem, beware
of the everything offer with little
or no teaching experience.

But one can relax because it pays
nothing, buy a hardcover book
with the proceeds, call oneself
a professional or a very educated person
with a lifelong hobby.

I told the man if I don't know I
will find out become an expert. Everyone loves
an expert, egghead not yet cracked
with indifference. Try to make people care
a little. But they are busy cutting their lawns
and nobody should bother them or maybe
the strangers are fellow church members, cars parked
in the grass, telling of a full house. The lottery bill
passed in North Carolina; they took a chance,
they bet on education funds and a guy
becomes broke wanting to be rich, rich
is it, it doesn't buy groceries, the money buys boats
and ambassadorships in record numbers, part
with rich money today.

If I don't know, I'll become an expert,
a bit overboard. It would be easier, community-like
to say "I don't know" and leave it at that;
that is the smarter thing to do
because you've left the teapot

on and are driving fifty miles per hour
down a city street
and lawyers are sending letters
to inquire
about the last ticket,
rolling through a stop sign
and leaving it upright
for the next person
to abide. So the teapot whistles
and I don't know anything
but Social Security Numbers
and bits from the past, flying
by like wind-driven stiff leaves
in autumn. It isn't okay
to be driven; I thought
it was for a brief time in youth
and then I needed to play catch up
for a long time, and it caught me finally
and I poured two cups of tea
and still drive very fast
because I like power on wheels, a V-6
with brakes all around. I've said it now
with the power of psychotherapy, discuss
your mother and your father
whoever else impressed childhood desire
of ponies and mini-bikes

of green bicycles
with shifters and passing time
with worms
before the rain, when a drop sent water circles
on the pond's surface.

I wait for rain and my menstrual period
both offering relief. I think
about words and loss
about how one can't make a profession
out of them by living them. It's fallacy,
a big mistake to think people ever mean
anything they say or would build temples
if words had power. Lawyers live
on words and blame comes their way,
too flimsy for foundations
too misunderstood to be credible.
A neighbor mows
the grass today; the grass is crunchy, the color
of a wheat field in sweet potato country,
the sweet potato is king here or is tobacco
the amber crowned wonder? I vote
for the wild flowers along the roadside
when the car is moving very fast
and the vision is fleeting, not confined
to elementary encyclopedias

from the 1960s. I wonder about
where things go before they're shut
in a white barn in Ohio. I wonder
if one can cry for not knowing
all that is lost, lost like a diamond
out of its prongs and panic strikes
but nobody cries over a fancy rock
laughable on the carpet assured
of eventual rescue, the dog knocks
it with a paw or the vacuum cleaners comes
so close.

I wonder where things go when they're not quite
gone, the lady with the special shoes
and bad thyroid talked about grieving
about crying in her office. Cry
about an illness and pray
and one knows ones already prayed
much about forgetting
and going on in that V-6
driving, wanting to drive
and to pray in hurricane season. I told
my friend to pray for the people in New Orleans,
and the water came, but it was storm surge
and not the blessing I ask for
when the water nourishes and brings life.

Today, I remember youth
and how nothing
seemed better
than dreams, better
than ability,
and somebody crooned
in an ear, a whisper
and I could do it my way,
one could make every colossal mistake,
overlook what bored
and sometimes
I could be haughty, the snob on call,
because dreams were brilliant
and I was smart, nothing better
to be.

"Smart" falters and still wonders
where these things go
when they're half gone
like the half glass of milk
after thick frosted cinnamon
rolls and you contemplate leaving
the rest or dumping it down
the sink when the guilt
of wasting food enters your mind.

Where do things go
when a trip is half over
and ones on ones way back
having seen tourists' sights
before, the museums,
the grown-over battlefields,
and restored celebrity homes
where the wife raised champion goats
and bragged that they had two udders
and produced warm buckets of milk
like in that Ohio barn
where calves have cream-colored
shag rug faces and well water comes
from a T-like spigot
in the farm's yard? I suppose
that spirited chickens, red chickens
or roosters run into the gravel lane
in front of heavy machinery
painted John Deere green
or International Harvester red
and the shops are nearly gone
where my grandfather cast tools
and made parts for 20 years
or most of a man's lifetime,
was nearly gone, half gone,
but such a man can go fishing

in travel trailers
to Canadian cool waters, large lakes
with loons and red and white lures
and white bent birch trees
where the bark pulls away like paper,
leaves blow like string mops
in the wind, half a wind going
somewhere, wherever things go
when kisses are far and few between
when every sweet word is asked
for and love is half, half love,
like a half note, has its own kind
of beat, and one can dance
however one wants under the moonlight
and I can concisely prepare
speeches and clever remarks
in case a stray listener is found
behind counters at the drug store
or feed store or hardware store. Imagine
the world, and it's full of listeners,
nobody talking, nobody being artful,
everyone has an ear to the garden row
and it smells in front of the white
Ohio farm buildings, the ground is dusty
and no rain will touch it, no rain can fall
today.

It does sprinkle, not buckets
finally wetting hanging leaves
and giving them pure courage
after WWII heroes are gone
and people can say they love,
promise forever
when the mood strikes
them and when the rain falls
the moon is full, going
away from the table, very fast.
It is not a dollar moon
or a dinner plate moon
or a globe cut out of paper
it is a moon with no comparison
and it shines after thunder surprised
the neighborhood, and folks rush
out to mowers and blowers
every engine howls
clippings will be sidelined
and everyone engages in lawn care.
I say it is a blessing when the moon
can only be described as a moon
and a white shed in Illinois protects
canisters of walnuts and wood handled hammers.
At the porch step a woman stands in a housedress

and warns us about the strawberries,
Don't step on them, let no shoes
come near but do crack
the nut with the heavy tool
and remember candy in deep pockets
of old men who loved children
and scare great grandchildren
with their wrinkles and soapy smell. Eat
mashed potatoes and listen to the mantle clock
the world is timeless and sleepy and bored
with so much adult talk. No room
is left unexplored, pictures of favorites
silver combs and stained glass, water from a pump
in the kitchen and the flooring is yellowed
and coals would burn hot if it were winter
in Illinois or Ohio where cars drive fast
and white-faced cows climb up a hill
from the creek. It is a blessing,
this rain opening memory
and taps the skylight when the house
is empty. It is gone now; I tried
to put it on paper and it resisted.
Do your words glide, do they skip,
are they easy on paper, do they tell me
anything I didn't know? It is okay to know
nothing. It is okay to push open that door

and make words sound against the frame.

Ohio

Are you smart, smartest now
and do your dreams
hit wooden porch planks and greet
me kindly like another scene
when mingling strangers
call and invite me
to churches or movies
or to sit in their living rooms?
Say I want nothing but words
and cars that go fast.
Say one is finally smart
enough to give up
every book, every common
quotation, every hint,
every clue. Indians
wait for rain in storybooks;
they dance, are festive.
Crops wait for rain. And the sea
is indifferent. The rain came and now
it has left. I'll wonder where things go
when they are half gone. I'll wonder.
ONE will make paper walls
and tear down wallpaper

The room will be white
like faces in barns and on steep hills
and beside rivers. The myrtle was late
in September and color stays
in one's mind, one's open mind, flooding
with images and people
from some other place.

Rain covers the street tonight
and yet it hesitates to fall
in large drops, drops that pound
against the windows and keep
one awake at night. The walker
does his round with an umbrella,
maybe a golf accessory
because of its blue and white stripes.
Earn your stripes and expect
a glorious heroes' welcome
for brawny carpenters working
in the aftermath of Katrina
or Rita. Ophelia left town before
too many talked about her;
she didn't have the force
to make the evening news,
too little destruction, blown-over
houses are newsworthy,

like the enlisted woman
from West Virginia who wanted
a college education and ended
up on trial for prisoner
abuse in Iraq, today
they arrested a fallen soldier's mother
for sitting close to the White House.
Crawford, Texas was her first camp,
her protest; she wanted someone to listen.
Imagine the world full of listeners,
broadcasters silent, lending
an ear to every hard luck story.
O'Connor says that "charity
is hard and endures." Watch out
for remarkable quotes
and people- who love wisdom;
they make no money
and are in the same cell
with Martha Stewart
and the mother who went political
at menopause. Today, scores
sit by televisions and say
she got exactly what she deserved
for expecting justice or for driving
fast to a not-quite Southern city
on the Potomac where somebody

crossed on a black clear night
or were there buckets of rain,
like a message to the other side,
a great leader is coming, great leaders
come and go in monument city
and well-dressed men dine
in expensive restaurants
because somebody else is picking up
the stapled tab, tabulation,
the tabulation is about a score
and winners are chosen daily
like a sweepstakes, like a prom queen
in the crocus tulip daffodil springtime
when the cherry blossoms
unfold in the capital city
before knowledgeable eyes? Never want
to know too much. Plead ignorance,
the Fifth, and don't ask me
to explain the Bill of Rights
or the Constitution
of brave men driving armored tanks;
the tank takes care of numerous concerns
and they will, I'll write home
for answers and instructions
for self-absorbed insights
about how I first began, how peace

ends and how silly men are elected
for four more years. Of course, I know
nothing.

Mt. Evans' hairpin winding curves
going up to the summit
and one can stand straight
at a slick paved lookout
and see no wandering buffalo,
maybe a few white goats
that nobody wants
in a windswept farmyard;
the barn is not open
this time of year
and thoughtless cows stand
in syrup brown grassy fields
and one might feel mountain air
from a high place
and remember unencumbered youth,
the freedom in not knowing
how quickly changes come and go
and I'll carefully pack that advice
with almonds and cashews,
with grain and white cheese
with less fat into a waterproof sack
because one could never imagine

poetry like this, or words put down
on paper lasting for more
than two thousand years, surely
they were drawn in pictures,
on smooth wet cave walls
and people were stick figures
without the power of reason. I'll
long for that black dirt because it's
something I can predict
in spring, summer, fall, winter
the only thing true happens;
in the now past, the moment
when I sat on a corner curb
and thought of existence
not because philosophy
was a discipline
but because I was tired
and needed to rest
with six-packs of empty
soda bottles and red cheeks
from exhaustion. What can
one ever understand about strong
minutes, short time when clarity
is overwhelming and baffling
and then startling back on two feet moving
to the grocery store?

An assistant in the editorial
department says in a boyish
voice, "We know you are looking
for something, so please know
this is a one time deal." Keep
looking, seeking, trying to find
what the mission essential is on earth
with its silver streaming sun
and turquoise Great Lakes
and slightly green ocean, salt
and rain leaves only salt water;
sailors put water in jugs along
with rum in case their fears ran
high after being on the ocean
for so long, looking for something
always mapping and dreaming
of solid footage, light shell-broken sand,
and fresh fruit or large nuts or berries.
They aren't ashamed that they
are looking, nobody can make
them feel bad about their quest
for survival when they're against
the storm, tempest sea; they
are not red-faced, red-handed;
they are not caught when trying

to make a living; they aren't pirates
but people with an ethic. Then go
to politically red Ohio, to the black dirt
and white faces tucked
into the barn; the barn door flew
open, and it wasn't a zipper down,
it was no joke; one can earn money
if one is willing to pay taxes, accept
tax cuts for the very wealthy; I'll
be in like Flint, Fred Flintstone
at the rock quarry. Carve everything
in stone. Carve your name. Etch
that you came to North Carolina
and became a seeker, looking
for authentic vocation, occupation,
a simple job on account
of multiple degrees; it is an ethic
to want to work in factories, in mills,
in furniture plants, but writers quickly
pass go attending real estate
class with fifty-something housewives
now working in department stores,
in cosmetics or fine jewelry
or household appliances with red plates
and mixers. It's the fate one has awaited
and it's waiting for me

if I lose several pounds and wax
two eyebrows, shapely and feminine. Words
won't work; they are only important
when they sell products like laundry soap.

Pull back. Words earn wages
for gabby indicted politicians
for morning editorial writers
who think great thoughts
and aren't busy in the afternoon
so they can chat
like a long distance phone call
from the lady in Ohio
or Missouri, from people
one rarely talks to and so share
details of shoe-buying sprees
and comfortable brands, high-class
shoes of poor quality, a worn hole
above the toe. Words are for hire
like carpet cleaners, tree trimmers
who know too that trees
aren't poems; the stately ones
fall come down for sidewalks
in front of homes, old
Friendly money mansions
with no young children

in sight; words are prosperous
in wills. claims, estates,
one will need to be exact
telling concisely what one means
to handpicked juries listening
to extents of injuries,
they're listeners, paid listeners
who fib out of duty
because they're busy mowing
lawns if they were not listening
to pitiful yarns stories
of unlucky plaintiffs
and resourceful defendants, words
can say when people witness
and remember details; the story
is made of accident reports
and fairies who see minutia,
a quick tip of a gray fedora
with a short red feather
from the strutting red rooster
let out of the barn
with advertisements on the sliding
door that slams against a frame
and close in, making insiders nervous
in small spaces without views
from the electric carnival rides, airplanes,

from scant air mountain lookouts,
from every high place
after the vision, the fast dream
on a sleepy morning in May; words
know what I'm thinking
once I find them; they tell
and they don't mind making salaries
if I'm very good, exceptionally
superlative fine or better than railroad
daring engineers when bandits
and masked men wanting treasures
for saloon gals, girls, women, ladies
and gentlemen come to the theater
to hear practiced lines
and to see well-timed tears
and they come to laugh deep belly
laughs and go home to silence
letting the yellow fat cat out
or hearing dogs bark
in the neighborhood. My words
have muscle, are strong
like malt liquor bulls
and champion herds moving
because the path is worn
to the barn, where buckets contain oats
and oats feed the young

on special occasions, when city visitors
come from far away. Words do
so much.

The teacher-poet taught
the many handout truth, a belly laugh
from the audience, clever reports.
I've heard that poetry deals
with the real tangible and abstract
in an imaginary way. Poets
are honest to a fault, the earth shakes
and heaves above them; California falls
into the ocean, a new coastline
is geologically formed overnight.
I've heard too much to tell exactly
what happened in the rural farmhouse
with the white barn, gossip
from little towns, villages
with uniform speed limits
for passing motorists. No one stays
at balcony shabby motels
or goes to the building downtown
to hear gray beat poets. The rooms
are unlighted; the guest poet corrects
practiced recited verse shaking his head
at mishap grammar in a key moment

when you are the word star
for being painfully honest.
The girl with the assistantship
says she doesn't believe
in any praise given in class; she
disagrees, she dissents
to pretty adjectives thrown
my way, disappointment
is mine and I can stuff
it into large fuzzy coat pockets
with bits of stray tobacco
and smoke on the steps
in winter, along
with the guy who never washes
his curly blond hair, and the women loved
him for his prose. Occasionally
he mattered, like all of us
looking for the mission essential
on earth, on any other planet
red or ringed with gases
where the people
have a few now minutes
and haven't evolved without ears.
The poetry class is extra
and nobody likes your real work
novel. Some are talking

of other lives, other circumstances
and who is to say if they lie?

Distant mild thunder sounds
like polished floorboards creak
at looking sleepless midnight
when the air conditioning turns on
and you're wide awake thinking
about day people's words,
in the dryness at the end
of the month; stagnant floods
are in New Orleans
and say that wasn't the rain
I intended with prayers, petitions
to a higher power, who sees all
knows all, and makes sense of the idea
that you know nothing, really zip
zero after years of education,
decades of experience
and a track record of being hardworking
and that's why one writes poetry
in silent afternoon, talking
about historical bandits
who jump between boxcars up
to the man with the safe's combination
or do they just blow the lock

to smithereens, to heaven?
Of course it falls back to the ground
a mangled mess
but the gold bars were fine
and worth their weight in butter
or is platinum the going concern
of prestigious credit cards,
meaning a borrower
makes oodles mega-bucks
and can't stay within a cash budget?
Don't worry about
accounts when words
can't pay rent or earn
a living wage. Bucks
aren't in the register, the till
like market bound white faces
coming in from rain;
it's pouring in OHIO, a deluge
too in mountain ranges for a few now
minutes, but one can't see it or feel
it because one stopped telling
the truth, worse yet admitting
it escapes when tightly pinned
down in a mile-long deep canyon,
not grand, just lost in doubt
and regret for trying to know

so much. The air is perfectly
still like people who are truly smart
and don't volunteer feeble nonsense.
Today, that word, a strong bull
intoxicating time-marker
makes one think what one said
was right on, was true, squirm
now or forever hold one's peace
squarely hitting straw targets
but please don't ever assert opinion
as truth. Opinions are for Saturday
newspaper readers, for cartoon lovers
gourmet bookstore coffee drinkers
featuring elephants and donkeys
with pack Native American blankets tiptoeing
around the steep turning ledges
and elephants carry Indian princes
through tiger jungles and crowded
roads.

Seekers

Truth gives one a soapbox
uneven letter activist's signs
and I can stand on the corner
and say loud bullhorn pontificate
to the harried unsuspecting

working world. It is embarrassing
to know so much for sure,
to be solidly convinced
with long passionate pleas
for others to follow
me who writes letters
to the editorial editor
even with the 30-day limit;
don't close fence me in;
I've an elaborate story to tell
and bystanders must listen
perk up ears to primetime political
speeches when approval
numbers are down, it must
make one down in the dumps
when one's sneaky sham rhetoric
doesn't sell and nobody believes
in what is put across
and the media corporation newspapers
don't mock but change
the subject when people
are about fed up, had it to here
on the wooden crate, speaking
high into the microphone.
Sages say it's never good
to be defended in a newspaper,

but Ralph Waldo
Emerson says don't worry
only bad repute is coming from people
who have made up their minds
from Ohio black dirt farmers
from church-going North Carolinians
from the Vermont Poet
Association where everyone
is glued to a seat with maple
warmed sugar; they're not happy
and the words are flowing
like hard water from the well
that white faces sip drink
after standing in the dry sun
from sunrise to sunset
and the form-conscious Vermont poets
could care less about Ohio
where ground is flat
like a deflated inner tube
and unchallenging
for gray-beard bicycle riders
who are also upset
in North Carolina
about a multitude of trucks
so be careful when one stands
in the street with a sign

be careful when I protest
fallen soldiers; some people
want sidewalks and on-time
school buses, want to fire
superintendents and defeat
board members at local dogcatcher
elections. And can I say
they lie? They know truth
about divesting stock, the truth
about Martha Stewart
at Camp Cupcake; they know
a thing or too about Enron
and bilking millions of pounds
of butter from retirement
accounts; but don't talk politics
unless one is prepared
for rebuttal; the therapist says
I can talk poetry, revealing
my innermost concerns
and don't say it has a thing
to do with the world
it's private, delivered
in a confidential letter
with CONFIDENTIAL printed
on the envelope; the truth
ran under the fence today again

and sleeps in a wingchair
upon designer pillow stacks
when nobody is looking
or is too preoccupied
to care about zealous school
board members in every town
the ones who graduated six children
from the system and know
everything for sure. Make
this person a friend, nod, eagerly
say "yes" and one is on the
way to never making another
wrong decision. Facts are involved
in decision-making. Emotions
make protest signs, travel to D.C.
to join with the Federation
to Free the Lost Seven, six or four
somewhere unfairly in rat hole jails
on the international scene.
I tell you citizens, registered voters
care when they know the truth
about one point stop sign ticket
or have tickets to swanky
sit-ins where Vermont poets
read from sunrise to sunset
and drink cool fruit juice

or martinis. I'm not telling
the truth because
Vermont poets do not leave
the Green Mountains
for country plaid furniture
or long uncomfortable tables
at dinnertime in winter let alone
for an outdoor festival; they're
words are classically eloquent
for nature and for mission
essential seekers who wait
for phone calls from books
editors who tell of the small
space on the pages; she'll look at it.
Essential seekers recite
resumes, vitas, emphasize
multiple degrees until they sound
against the frame, pathetic
in their own minds; so they
comfort soothe themselves
with the thought of being
the word star anyway, I'm
the word star on an important
journey, sending out poet honesty
to deadline workers
who aren't fond

of being bothered between
abrupt answers. O' pity
where did you go? I thought
you were half gone
like the heavy cloud cover
in the Carolinas today, that
intoxicating, vodka, kick-ass
word strikes again
with so much spunk
and urgency, today I saw
the light, knew the truth
in now moments, for a short
minute in a Piedmont village.

He says that I'm a ffffine writer
so you go to the empty October beach
in a road rough silver sports car
to find the beach windy
and the boats coming
into the marina. The sea
is olive drab green
and the horizon is periwinkle
like a rich man's middle name
a funny word, a nerd word
as I note land shelves, erosion
from the last hurricane

that took a couple
of shingles from a rentable
house with a walkway made
of treated wooden planks
one can know for sure
that one needs a vacation
are tired of sweet penniless
words; you were going to say
it is a blessing and it is a blessing
when the mood hits
to express yourself
to voice someone else's opinion
as long as there is an agreement
so a man with integrity
can stand at a podium
before a cheering
and applauding crowd. Tell
them the nation
is going to change,
is going to become fair
and just, just and equitable
like the Founding Fathers' idea
that all men are created equal;
the balance of the scales
of justice, the lady
with her bronze dress

open at the top, sexy, blind
reassuring downtrodden
peoples everywhere. The
beach was a vacation three
Eastern hours from home
where the dog
is tightly caged from growth
and cars are the buzz
with engine lights on
and three designer pairs
of soft cased sunglasses
in the locked glove box,
where letters
are occasionally welcomed
along with bills
in the bush-covered mailbox
and the sky turned aqua
above the horizon;
the sand wouldn't pack
but was loose, and we watched
the sandpiper's skinny legs go
back and forth; sometimes it
finds a shelled morsel
with its black pencil beak
and nods to the lazy pelican
beside us, and the thought

of word failure doesn't leave
my mind but camps out
with a bright burning fire
hot, high, dangerous
to think too much
about inadequacy,
about the fabulous things
one might do if one were
a tangled beard pirate
with short blue pistols
just back from a raid
and noisy coins
run through thinning
fingers, hands with jeweled rings
full of meaning, a life
so full of meaning,
and happenings not understood
but accepted, accepting county
fairs where men put out political
buttons in reds, greens,
and yellows, bumper stickers
show from rusty chrome, metal
indicating social status
or how much one is worth
after raiding government coffers
or the king's treasure chest,

after being shipwrecked
and tossed to sea landing
on an island with other mates
people who do not count
anymore, and I can say
that's not true, everyone votes
in democracy, in Walt Whitman's
aggregate religious society
more than a hundred years ago
and I wonder if belief
is cut in stone, if it was strong
like white face bulls
in Indiana, show me Missouri
or Wisconsin where statesmen
are progressive, buying homemade
fatty cheeses and footballs tickets
for a Northern team snowing
hometowns for Vermont poets
who never write propaganda
if they can help it; they're steeped
in tradition attending Robert Frost
meetings for writing societies.
The ocean is olive green,
the color of army uniforms
and rolls, slides, foams
back and forth to make-believe

justice because anything
is possible in the face
of beauty, and nature,
and God, that higher power
that lets one know one cannot
tell the truth on one's own
I cannot count on pirates
and railroad bandits
or people with integrity
when given mucho power
within the military industrial
complex, that 1950s, 1960s
stuff that applies
to a world losing compassion
and experience, and eloquent
Vermont poets who
are seldom political, in now time
until the times call prophets
and others of important words.

So you scribble an address
on a losing candidate's notepad,
sending out another resume
for thoughtful consideration
and I wonder why politics
pursues me and won't let

me turn away to a farm
or an ocean, petrified sharks
teeth are out the question
and now three years from fifty
I've many inquiries
to make of noteworthy men
who succeeded today
realizing mission essential
the same year seminary
was plausible
believable in my mind
and again I knew the truth
again for a month, a year,
in the daytime or nighttime;
something made me think
I could tell others
and I was wrong
while others were winning
prizes, exacting salaries,
and gaining titles
to impress investors too
material for truth. Wrong
can be absolute; I don't
need to be reflective, at some point
there is sabotage always
observations too keen for men

keeping jobs, passion
is scary to well earning,
excitement is for baseball games
where the bases are loaded
and the ocean is exquisite
to me, too amazing to be believed
too energetic, moving, swaying
making its point to me
without words, but I insist
and so come up with colors
and names of birds
because I've have to urgently
need to go back to Victorian
kitchens and a grandfather
that didn't drive to New Boston
drinking beers instead. Go
back to some root, an anchor
for pirate fantasies,
like one ever had a name
and needed a millions words
to make fuel take-off, lift-off,
whatever makes one go very fast
to fickle planet stars, fate destiny,
obsession, illness, and staying
within bounds, avoiding tickets
now.

The rain comes down for two days now. The illness scares me
and makes me wonder
about the future. I think my commentary is too liberal for
North Carolina papers. The audience is different than in the
Midwest also. I think they're more passionate, and
so are more difficult to get along with. But 1960s' liberalism
is out; it's unlucky to be
out of sync with the times. Minimalism went out with
Raymond Carver, and probably
will soon be back after college instructors have told students
to stress details. Details are all.

Adrienne Rich warned about silence
of its peril and she is right, correct, aye
to count the tremendous cost,
to pull out her international Visa
saying I can't pay cash
today. I can't come up
with president profile nickels and quarters
dimes: forget the pocket change
everyone wants new dollars
the monetary revolution
when slight hungry children
aren't fed, drugs cost too much
and are like unanswered silence

but it's not quietness
we pay for; it is the knowing
the same thing the first
human beings cast out for paper.
It is often knowing when situations
are wrong misunderstand the television image
trying paper bills, legal tender money
that can pay for substandard housing
shacks for rough roofs, noisy hot water pipes
for blue smoking air out of climbing stacks
with lights so airplane pilots
are sufficiently warned about colossal structures
about possible collisions midair tragedies
fog-related accidents earth revolving
so populated without caring kin
and others who can be called
in a tight pinch, when chest pains
and other physical body maladies
are the battle of the day
and we know solitary nothing
of time and her plans
and we can break the silence
but we can never pretend
to tell the truth, we can only know
half of the price and even Rich
says, she contends take it or leave it

the toll is inevitable while one wonders
about the steady rope stream of rain
in the concrete gutter moving
to where rushing drain water goes
after blinding downpours
after the holy deluge
nothing but record weather events
for days, nothing but subzero
for muted Moscow, for once warring Berlin
and passionate Russia cuts back oil supplies
for Finland: the message is
come along, cooperate or else wear
authentic fur muffs and scarves cover
the stinging faces of Red Square
and Cossacks in wool trousers claim
to absolutely know there
and of course knew nothing
but political doctrines and ideology
a nineteenth century manifesto for workers
when white dusty block ice is measured
in feet, in meters, and thickens
and people who knew
the exacted price of knowing what
was not popular and protests
not necessarily spoken, put on signs
but shown in giveaway glances

informed eyes are poor liars
even when they need
to be dull and stupid disinterested
bargain hunters bystanders making their way
to meat markets, the string tag shows.
Landscape planters are full
of dead resting leaves in January
and the strong lasting summer
will soon come with its lifted
bully heat; it is the season I dislike
the full weighty trees wilt
and people wear fringy straw hats
at noon in the middle of the day
like Asian peasants in a rice field
and the African air sweeps across
the Atlantic swirling
like a spoon in a coffee cup
or ideas on an anxious night
and all finally passes with the day
memory recollections of former
of history personal leather interiors
driving time into the future
as if it were a groove-wheeled tractor
in a muddy competition to pull
another at the fairgrounds
of youth a rodeo breaking bronco

and milky mashed potatoes
from the Presbyterian women under
a rust-colored canvas tent; the hucksters call
from chance game rows and everybody
wins today a teddy bear if one can look back
with clarity, with visual acuteness
or make sense of where one's
been in pink shaded houses with sidewalks
near grocery and drug stores
a mile away from the community
gem college, the Swedish
institution with anemic white faces
and proper well-spoken professors
tell texts and who know Shakespeare
in a farmer's, tiller's city
and the black rich earth until
we understand local history too
the land value corn crisp
making dark night rustles
in the July summer wind
worth large faded overalls on
callous skin muscular hands
weathered men talk at the feed storage
centers grain elevators and recount
other harvests sending children
to limestone pricy private colleges

so they can come home
and nobody understands farming
or philosophy but knowing
is the goal of worn fathers dutiful
and round mothers who staking
pride and stewing apples
for meals chicken fresh
eggs in the morning coffees houses
and guitar sessions in another
world that she brought life to
in birthing labor and see the hands
that know the azure earth safety
in knowing how vegetables
grow and how seedlings sprout
at noonday cold bundled against
elements without chemistry
or tabs calculations; how we
calculate and perfectly envision
the future expecting grass
to grow high ground cover in cooler spring
and love, sacrifice faith, pleasing
theater movies that do not last long
blue collar workers build portfolios
and anticipate falsely government
checks and will pay health
care life car insurance as the way

we live next to knowing
sweetly endowed Swedish colleges
we will be secure realizing
the sixteenth century artwork masters
seven naked ladies posing with cherub
from another era, the hot
flat summer will not be a friend
when the garden becomes dry
that is the cost of homely revolutionaries
of who reckon with wooden-handled hoes
and simple pruning autumn tools
and take defiance out in yard work.
An outreaching child will come home
and know more than generous parents
and that's the way life progresses
leaving solid legacies we call tradition
nothing changes from this equation
the oppressive heat is for six months
and it is the cost, the copper penny price
for lamb winters where the rain
falls instead of snowflakes.

I do not know Vermont poets
You can't say I'm guilty or complicit
or good enough to write verse for critics.
I don't know them so I imagine

that their rugged in-tune children grow up
to be ardent environmentalists
sitting in meeting halls with painted floors.
I don't know if stiff winter winds
blow through estate houses or if wood burns
cut from gray rust rotting trees, trees dead
and long stretched out across soft forest bottoms.
I can't be faulted for not knowing their choice
of drink simple dinners because we can only imagine
our closest or farthest neighbor we think
about weighty prestigious university theories
on how the earth turns, about religious texts
and we guess on the most important
aspects of existence and easily call out
and speak of inculcating knowledge to young
unthinking students dulled from images
unrelated to matching words with their objects
and now they don't understand us
we don't understand what modern media marvel
is in their brain. I only know what I read
in the newspapers. I only know what I hear
on television and the world splits in its sources
back to the dense machete land and the longest river
and indigenous drums, customs that mean
nothing to us. I wonder about your truth
that you write on the afternoon freight trains

by broken windows in a government legislative
building. I wonder if you've heard
we do not negotiate bargain play easy
with guns and now people silent; what do they
think? What are they suppose to say
in houses rubble in streets crooked
in fenced in areas where people spend their time
all day all night weeks months lifetimes
in wrecked ruined bulldozed shattered houses?
I do not know Vermont poets or the scope
of their concerns. Frosted apple orchards
are near ice glazed windows without storm glass
when the harsh season is boundless. Are poets'
clothes mimicked in catalogues and mail order
online and shipping costs rise and I've given
a credit card number for a chamois-like shirt
in heather? I told you I know nothing
about northern culture do not hesitate to speak
because ignorance assumes before it knows
without fully exacting the price of delivered goods
or services. Vermont poets are prophets with right
deep words and forceful lines. I think they might move
us even push forward if anybody heard their lines
almost too English pretty, but not too pretty if everyone
understood words. Authentic bards poets
talk to themselves and do not look

up words in the dictionary; its too late for that
meanings aren't universal and I, a Midwestern
poser: I might claim to know audiences,
but I only guess about Vermont poets.

I can only suggest they are not books.
Books are like years ago college friends
I expect nothing from them but a message
once a year when I remember sage whispered
thoughts coming into my ears like welcomed
waited for stories displayed on magazine racks
at the newsstands where people sip hot potent
bitter cups without liquor.

I occasionally want
a hefty volume to make me drunk with another's
words, falling down drunk when the keys are taken
away or hidden under the straw mat on the step
put above a narrow weathered doorsill.
I want books to reveal what I have never thought
of like how to scuba dive in paradise
how to change an overdue timing belt
how to cook for perfectionist chefs
for frequent restaurant goers fine suited
New York investors who keep the bottom line
and wear dime store reading glasses.

I often haven't read books
in a linear way looking for what startles
amazes like showy silk clad magicians
at advertised circus performances
high wire acts acrobats defying gravity
and planning for the future like seers.
I want books to tell me that I feel kinship
with the universe with cosmic hippies
and people considering what
it means to be at a crossroads turning
very fast in one direction skidding
on the brown puddle pavement
exacting speed space valorous intent.
I expect much from books
but I do not want them to sing melodies
or do things that are not for them.
I do not want them to plant radishes or tend
babies in the afternoon. I do not want
them to switch the shining river's direction
or make ponds fill into anglers' lakes.
I want companions with limits scope
describing planet Neptune journals
of scientific men agreeing with poets fine
about the moon starlight night words
at their best and books finally retire
go to sleep in board made shelves white

seen from the street in vague pictures.
I do not want to know everything they tell.

I do not know laboratory scientists
who might wear white coats
or beige Dockers. I could not understand
their articles on stem cells global warming
inescapable climate change. Their forecasts loom
for poll driven politicians to ignore the heating earth
for memory-lapsed middle-aged onlookers who never
believed in the establishment status
when they were young out of the slick
university tiles polished during lull times
when the students were in bars lifting
beers and preparing for tests. I imagine
scientists like poets have followers
and they walk down the hall with protégés
and assure them about graduate schools.
I understand nothing about tables. I guess
that scientists are masters of small talk;
esoteric experiments far out and not meant
for truck drivers, dry cleaners, workers
so they talk about hamburger joints
and write graph-filled papers that journalists
sleepily decipher after deadlines. They talk
about cat dog family pets and know nothing

about each other; the biologist is distant
from the methodical chemist and the weatherman
is not an astronaut. The drugs made today
will make you predictably sick with side effects
but the alternative is being sick
so FDA officials stamp approval
on high pressure systems mumbo jumbo
to increase credibility and ongoing belief
in the guess.

I do not wish to be known like mice
when the black yellow razor beak hovers above
circling the clandestine musings in town speak
about where you came from with your fake
country accent.

I did not come from a farm
in Ohio, and I do not know white faces
in the river valley where I used to play
in the hours before dark. Cows stood
on the river's steep flood eroded edge
and looked on at the boat, the city's
lights colored the water for miles. You
can be known for great talent
even talent finds its enemies
because it is dangerous to stand out

the patterned butterfly is pinned and cased
for elementary children and no one ask
whether it should've been special unusual
Know it might have said yes for short glory
the bright moment when a concise word hits
the page, the arrow pierces targets
and love is returned. I do not know
if glory is worth a pound of green grapes
on sale in the summer market. Glory
deceives the one who jumps into battle
and only half dies with useless legs
so much for courageous intent
and the dreamy butterfly knows the cost
of flying into nets, the cage, prisons
of being closed into the barn awaiting
a trip to the feed pens; young white faces
are kin to beautiful beings fate deals
a losing tragic lot and they no longer climb
hills in illusions of freedom unheard
of fences in ephemeral awareness.
I 'd rather have a pound of grapes
than appear to have knowledge
in front of those who confidently
expound spin speaking as broadcasts.
Still I might put my grapes into a basket
and imagine a light wine

a wine that is not troublesome
making every occasion a celebration.
I do not know but I can hope
like the slightly living rose bush
in February. I can hope to remember
trying events and travel destinations
of exactly how my life has unfolded
of how I have missed out lamenting
miscalculations destiny errors as if one
affects a journey through space and time.

I want to sleep on rainy nights only hearing
the drops cover the green stems
of spring waiting. I want you to ride in my car
and never question the speed of
a heist-like getaway. The world revolves around
the sun keeping equilibrium in its hurried
pace. I see no reason to stay in place
awaiting Midwestern scenes. I tell you
now that we can love and not know. It's
the simplest endeavor and requires little
reflection from burning stars. One can
await uniformed couriers delivering books
letters from overseas and watch as they go by
speeding in secure trucks backing
into driveways rushing to doors with large

packed boxes. Come with me now, today
and let's be heroes recognizing
when the wasted undeclared war is lost
whatever we imagined will not happen
here and there is no point in staying
to look at missed opportunities.
I cannot wonder about how time links us
to fads so one is outdated and comment counts.
But come with me today seeing a strong
common word show its urgency. Ah, we are alone
you say and ancient philosophers sit on stumps
while bony romantics disagree seeking
to cover up that passengers are moot
and harbors are unsafe when booted pirates
whittle whistles to call on thugs. Come
with me now today; this is the now verse
and these words this jazz is not wisdom
can only suppose the workings tacked
to the board. If we're alone there is pretense
and we can live out vineyard patience while
darkness sweeps the gray from twilight
hours, and I show you all I've witnessed
about home.

I do not know Ohio farmers. I see them
riding tractors across fields from the road.
I suppose the land is a legacy, and the farmer
calls his tract home. It is where animals
are animals without sentimental ownership
or names. They come and go to sustain permanence
lifestyles. Cats are special and live in sliding door
barns to keep down mice birds unsuspecting.
Farmers are kind in their own way never shying
away from pragmatism and know what needs
to be done for the day. I do not want pragmatic
love scripted and without nonsense. A time
without folly should be short laughter persists
throughout trials when the mind could turn
as rough as skin weathered in the drying wind.
I don't know that for sure. I see these people
with simple political opinions; they visit
with elected officials at county fair booths
and never think of Lincoln or Grant or civil
wars the past is gone to farm workers tilling
land as flat as an ironing board. If they are
in trouble the community exists as a yesterday
prop. I guess they suspect they are as alone
as twentieth century thinkers but they do not think
these thoughts when the hay is cut.

Small Boats

I can tell you about my home grown over
and a grapevine tangle on the single wire fence
and nobody farms and nobody answers phones
or doorbells. People walk in and leave messages.
I can tell you I learned football plays in the side
lot and took V-bottom boats to where the river
was encroached with poplars and it gave off reflections
of its dense borders. I followed the pastimes of old
men who lived in unpainted porch- covered cabins
and caught catfish. I did not know them but heard
their names from others. Small boat motors
were on stands waiting for repair, and I waited
to leave, read books to leave, imagined the life
of an educated recluse with no pond. When
I came back I claimed nothing and wore white
blouses and yellow shorts gave up sweatshirts
and for a while I could not love the river. I could
not love the past and it was gone.

I take everyone I love there.
It's a precedent and they stand
on a concrete seawall seeing the sights
freedom and discontent. I think they should visit.
Water laps the blowing wind makes the river
run backwards. Currents take one away

and one cannot swim against broad
motion never ceasing never apologizing
for carrying trees like Viking ships.
I want you to know the cost in slime mud
in landmark dive tavern marinas blistering tar
roads. I want you to come with me
when we leave and guess a leading part in a play
in another time. Distant past is theater.
It wins an award for just showing up
in altered evening gowns prom dresses
below a massive chandelier. I find my ideas
for books here preserved for onlookers during
floods rough-sided jacked-up houses built on stilts.
We can go now to jewel Swedish colleges
and try to know diagramed botany, the lesson
of plant fertilization and children myths.

Happenings go without musings
and leave dryness, dusty, unobserved
events and inadequacy is felt, in memory
in stilted words coming too easy. One can rage
against flint hardness, the sharp callous scope
of numerous chatty witnesses, of numerous
buzzing injustices mounting abstractions
confusing staying with one's sentences
until the end of sighing. I can tell you

I've tried too hard, stout romance's puppet
for three decades. It's not so simple: someone
should have said loudly after tapping rapping
my strained head and hearing its brains clatter
in the cupboard where I keep the big tea
cup with authors' faces; their names
below the image. I do fault the paper
for not making people understand what
it took to get to the office supply store
origins are unimportant matters. Yesterdays
are for thin-lipped historians smoking pipes
in rising blue compartments for buffs touring
the long line of monuments and camera-clad
tourists aiming focus on gossipy war boots
and a broken dish.

I do not blame time. Time is innocent
like the full chalky blackboard waiting
to be erased so eager teachers can start over. I
see no earthly reason to pick on space;
there is only so much room; greedy intellects
take it all like the bank robber when the vault
opens and there is small quarters to fill
the leather suitcases and catch the train
out of town before the law comes down hard
searching streets alleys car lots restaurants.

Cops want the paper and to give back what
was stolen from another. Relics recall
when the money is found ten years later
underneath the rose garden at the corner
church. I say you can fool bad guys
and good guys as a collective because paper
can't help it but it lies and never knew the truth
while the lights shine through a tree encircled
neighborhood yard owned for ten years
by a freewheeling chemist and his wife.

Bandits are a Hollywood construct
like deer pioneer ice statues in Minnesota's
warmest January. We see the tugged at
loss and claim fiction yarns tales make believe
when we know we could never let any
of it go on our own. We couldn't say "Take
it," I am glad. The man with the covered
face and short gun is part of our imagination.
I do not know him; his essence slips slides
when broad yellow rays heat pavement
turning playful faces red so that they blister
after the mild short months after New Year
in St. Paul or Minneapolis or near boundary
waters where metal bark canoes are carried across
boggy woods onto another nameless lake

and the untested water is fine for drinking
and food is put in the trees at night so bears
thieving animals don't take it in the dark.
I do not know thieves or what they want
with paper backed up by the treasury, what
they want with paper for business newspapers
telling of American carmakers lay-offs. I see
paper when orders are decreed and when
accounts are settled little slips and when the
carwash accepts certain codes. I've seen hideous
blank paper try to negotiate with timid words
held to their surface; the words want off
good bye because sense tells that communication
isn't a primary job and no one
will want packed sentences of the robbed
because of well placed letters. Words are solitary monks.

I've never seen a pirate; one supposes they steal
from government ships, the King's ship
and some royal Navy officers swing down ropes
wishing not to walk the plank. The plank
strikes me a bit odd but it is the nautical movie
way men are punished on boats. One supposes
too that they are chained below until wrists bleed
and the pirates claim victory after treasures
are opened which might be hearts if the measure

weren't gold. I've multiple degrees loving words
and word stars from poetry class and everybody
oohs and ahs when they do the dance today
and knives aren't between the teeth and poets
don't fear drowning but the dead silence
of disapproval after one drives very fast
to school contemplating an audience of
young people. I'll be their matronly aunt
and know why red apples are red
and turnips are like white and purple radishes
and they will mock me when the hour is over
for saying too much about scantily dressed
pirates living near the water and poets living
by the water catching the surf yet another way
to walk the plank turning tan while marine
biologists collect samples of sea water testing
its saltiness. I'll be the old salt man fishing
from the pier and students assume I know
tides and little else beyond the illness in my knees
and they will ignore me until I'm featured
in verse. I'll be the child lost in motion
carrying sand buckets and laughing
at waves unaware of pencil-legged birds
and parents smelling of lotion and beer. I
will never be the point of a poem because
the poets are young and children are distant

ideas not yet full of pathos. I think I know
young poets, but you've probably guessed
that I lie like paper unwilling just to stop
to quit saying like Vermont elders
who are the prophets and would never write
about being the old woman in a
large family picture, but one can hear
much when one is invisible; the people
do not mind speaking and they do not mind
outdated kin who couldn't tell the names
of pop stars and who don't know what's going
on in Manhattan, the latest in rent
or what people do in a city what they do
in the country after they've fled
to a better location. The tide comes in
and I sit on the apartment rocks
with my almost multiple degrees dreaming
of time and how she's always a girl busy
with retreating sand and nets
for nothing but the fall of water through the weave
no prison, no chains, no plank, a linear
rush, a straightforward movement without regard
or care. Time visits paper and leaves the doors
open, the dishes out, the bed undone forever.
And poets will wince but that is the cost
of imagining against something as real

as time and the messy houseguests whose
prints are on the floor in Georgia red mud
of the clay pot persuasion, Cherokees on
their way from home. I can't say for sure though.

Specialist doctors say they don't know for sure
reading MRIs and ordering blood tests.
Uncertainty suspends illness in thought
while it exists in a body losing its health
and I can drive very fast down curved
tobacco two-lane highways, very fast
never knowing if one can negotiate
the sharp turn with a full-sized automobile
from Wendover. I feel like I could tell
you what I want from words now
and I might fail to give them due respect
deserved honor because of my own inability
to say it right. My perception isn't clear
and I think I've been discouraged
about their uses in the world; words work
from fire stations, with elevated electrical
workers. They're prominent in hospitals
and other places where people utter
needs, requests for healing. I see flocking birds
as a sign of holiness and wonder why the scenes
matter to me. Doves and white pigeons

both stretch gliding across
state lines interstates are not the easiest
way to go fast, for words to tumble, going
on their ends to create understanding.
I saw a retriever watch a quail from a window
intently, never taking its eyes from the bird
and they might have been friends, and they
might have stayed in the backyard woods
if the hunter did not come between them.
Our instincts look for healing, words
are the arbitrator and go into
whatever madness we've adopted
in the beating heart on road abandoned Sunday
when small buildings ring
and gladness touches souls and other real
notions like sturdy faith that can only
be to the grasping keeper like the eyes
holding the keen hunter's prey on the post.

I went back, turned back, a pilgrimage, a way
to childhood roots, the stained glass,
the curved door, heavy dark wood
where the saints formerly lived
with their weighted drape-like robes
and calm somber expressions
as if they knew they were the church's

chosen. They have to be good and perform
a miracle. They were the examples, models
for young people who were impressionable
and thought that holiness
was as long and shadowy
as beams across the sanctuary.

I went to the grotto, where a Hispanic woman
and a five year-old saw the Virgin Mary
\and told the newspaper; people came
from miles around filling the parking
lot of a riverfront restaurant. The cameras
descended, and some said they saw nothing
but were believers, others want to believe
like I do in more than ordinary life,
the blue robe Our Lady of Lourdes, Our
Lady of Kernersville and Moline,
every miscellaneous town along the river
and along the interstate who makes
herself known for celestial purposes
who rarely visits for naught. I prayed
to her after penance, as a child
can admit error, mostly made up,
mostly surfacing in adult life
for truth because nobody likes it
and eventually the truth makes its path

into light. It comes to where others
can see it, and there aren't apologies,
except those given on steps in front
of three-storey brick school buildings
and perhaps one will have to testify
and maybe not. It is nice to be trusted
again after years, after the time
goes by and a young woman writes
and comments about news stories.

I used to know but cannot claim
truth now after the swirl of color
after the many, many squares
of retold stories put together
with what? I guess glue or steel
or lead or invisible words,
pictures without words. The
cross stands out, the Catholic
grandmother who believed
that everyone had something to bear
and unbelievers can be unbelievers
because catastrophe doesn't happen
and men escape the meaner qualities
in living, the poor are devout
in foreign countries where wealth
is not and too obvious, where cars

and four bedroom homes
aren't in real estate sections
for all to see, admire until
witnesses are sick with inadequacy
and greed. My faith is resilient,
weathers the speeding wind
that blow down parts of weaker trees
leaving the trunk and spindles.
I've tried to take hold of this feeling
when the soul is placid and all
is well and all shall be well
when the grotto Lady stands
under the lights of the river
a playground, where the catfish's
smooth skin slides through
water and people are brought home
to look. Oh, but we can't be sure.

We can't sure about any particular holy
place among sinners; then where
should the truth come? Who needs
love more than drunken fools
and riverboat captains, the gracious
servants who are lost in business
who would come home if they were called?

I gave my mother a rosary
and she said it was to her liking
with iridescent beads aqua and green.
I wonder what she thought
on that Good Friday, her face said
she was full with unexpressed words
the sounds we hear in our minds
the sorrow we do not share
the love we've perhaps forgotten
in rituals and pageantry in being
with others who might suspect
our uncomfortable seat before
the Lord. Yesterday I slept all day
and was up at mid morning. I make
no sense of the hours unconsciously
spent in riddling dreams
and afterthoughts and no way
to drive home with the roads
jammed with trucks. The risk
might be worth it through mountains
driving fast, keeping steady, and
why does no one call when half
applauded and the other half were
silent? If they called would they say
that they missed me, would they call
me talented, brilliant and it was

a mistake to force me out even though
I quit? I want the audience to know
what plain darned happened and why
I put down my pen and why
I want the porch light on
in the summer, so people can see
through the thick trees. I tire
of looking through window glass
and seeing only various green, only
the two mini-vans and a woman
gardening with yellow gloves.
I drink coffee now and the teapot
is still and whistles no more. The
world should know, this knowing
is important, is crucial, is exacting
but I cannot tell you anymore.
I planted grass seeds in the springtime,
more green, and I long for the
colors and a horizon, a large sky,
with brown, and faint sunshine on
white hay. You tire of my homesickness.
It is all I shall speak of now. I've done
the national lecture circuit to applause
and find I want to go home
and rest without a special name
but as one who has worked hard

and as one who has given while
others have been professionals
and secretaries, have typed a million
words and have loved a dictionary.
I want precisely not to be rich
but to carry daily food to two dogs
who sit outside my door waiting
for human contact. That will not
be much to ask in the future.

Today, I decided that I want
too much, indifferent time ticks on
and stop it or control
what it gives. Time never promised
me anything so why should I be dismayed.
It is not the slightest trouble
that the clock's hands move around
forever, never noting that people
observe when they move past a number
and peace could happen today,
if leaders willed it so. The killing
could stop in days, in hours, in minutes
if the right minds willed it with black
neckties and state plates, long speakers
until everyone wanted to go
home, resting, retiring, giving in

to gray clouds of smoke
the bargaining red chip
on the shiny smooth floors
of deadly remembered malls
and swanky restaurants.
Today I thought it might begin,
the silence of a rising mood,
the hot tangled but cold rubble
powder ashes tired and without heat
or life whatever moves a person
to pity or repugnance over loss.

Creeds

The kitchen television was silent
and no news came, no mouth
spoke creeds and declared opinions
until the cord spit from the wall
about all the knowing
and pretending that people
do when they cannot know
for sure. I can talk like
that and show off my language,
verbs spew from my tongue
and I understand action,
what soldiers do on alley streets
and from vacant buildings.

I know the papers that are signed
under light blue ties and flag pins
for the betterment of the ages,
action, I might understand it
if it were well intentioned
and for restoration, a return
to what used to be in public affairs
when food was plenty, abundance
was in the pantry, in drawers
with clean socks and in gas guzzling
SUVs. I only know what we used
to know and now it does not pertain
to the present or history
but forward events marking
the bounty of dreaming consumers
picking up where someone left off.

Mighty Israel is defending itself
with forward movement
and the world watches the rockets
hit Lebanon. All concrete crumbles
in front of the global community
and we are shocked at destruction
and detached, and far away, dry
faced and the interested parties
know one poisoned truth or a another
one story or a couple. Who can

say? Who will say which country
intrudes invades marches into
foreign lands? It is too much
and one should never want
for the birds to know how badly
the earth is torn. Time let us rethink
the possibilities, an alternative
to bloodshed for real, like when
the mockingbird sings in the night
and the chickens come home to roost
and when the robins return in the spring
and the bluebird makes its country home
you will see beyond the devastation
and your occupied mind will suppose
that it knows the fair sky
where creatures fly wanting nothing
but abrupt change, revolution
of beginnings of quietness
and well being or health away
from the desire to speed past
blacktop highways and yellow
line and they want sweet ample rain.

The bucket-poured rain is overlooked
and cannot cool the burnt earth
when weather is not a problem.

Don't complain about heat any longer
unless your heart is stone broken
into sand, like in the towel
of a beach bum. Shake it off,
the problem, the approved carnage
washes like the sea, seeming natural
to those who watch the waves
arrive with more and more power,
the ability to carry or drop aquatic life
in its tedious rush. The sea
is bored with breathing objects.
You foolish children wade out deep
as if some tender eyes protected or
even cared. Run with presumption,
scurry off quickly from false lovers
and journalists with right and left-handed pen.
Take your trust with you. I could call
you out and we'd keep our pistols in a
velvet-lined boxes and then we'd walk ten
paces and turn, fire, and, fall, then we'd stand
up again and repeat the silly game
because our leaders aren't statesmen
in motorcades; we are just playing a game
like they are tinkering with death
and who they call does not stand up again.
There is no comfort in war. We can only

stand far enough away that we can pretend
not to know the damage. This is great
advantage to contrived stupidity; we
aren't made to show disapproval
and say we are innocent and perhaps
we are for never pulling pins
or planting mines, for never launching
a missile. Our hands are clean, our laundry
is stacked in piles away from the commotion
the locomotion of explosive events
and revenge.

I'm bored with green. I admit that my car
goes too fast. I'm homesick and am
without position. The poet has no place
in the world besides Vermont, and I've told
you about that. My words baffle me, and I doubt
their verity. I like rain and to talk about birds
and dogs. I go back to Catholic grandmothers
and talk about truth, have the guts
to summon the word, call it up
like it were a spirit. I tell you over and over
again that I can't say for sure and know very
little. Have you loved me for this?
Do you understand me, putting it all together?

My long poem, my discourse, my treatise, is too
heavy but I will lightened for you, whom I
do not know and cannot name. I will speak of clarity
and show you the greatest boldest river
in the dew morning when it is as flat
and as mysterious as a film negative. Water
falls from my fingers and drops freckle
my hands. There are no drunken captains
but gentle old men who fish on the riverbanks
with worms from under the abandoned plywood
in a grown-over lot. The lot is tame though
and nothing that lives there bites, like you
complain of the melancholy in my verse.
Do you remember loving a man, a woman,
or some commitment that would last?
Did you ever put a ring on your finger? I think
you like the way ice cream runs down a
cone and the squirrels that hop from the
trash bins at a favorite university. I think
you are probably kind, bald, growing bald,
and somebody's uncle. I will not make you real
because I want you to hear me out and I'll try
to make it all more pleasant, and I'll not talk
of war.

There is a ceasefire and sides claim victory;

people wait out the silence to see if its true,
if the bombs stop dropping and soldiers stop
falling. I told you there be better news if you
could wait. People sigh and children are found
in the streets still wandering orphans until
somebody finds them. I promised you a happy tale
and I'm a tale-teller. I haven't one scent of
your favorite aroma. I cannot give you what
you want most: words that don't cheat. You
want to hear clear bells pealing for towers
on university campuses and she said she'd call
but hasn't yet. I won't wait by this phone
for it betrays me with a foreign voice
a person who wants me to consolidate my college
loans, neat like the sundial on a shady day. I tell
you on a day when the sun shines time
is eternal and no trickster. The phone offers
a cheery voice but tells no jokes, seldom
laughs aloud or reads verse to me. What use
is it then? It is to sit by, to carry and ring
in the parking lot. The war is over
and now there are only telephones to worry
us, to go off in some chosen melody when
driving very fast to the place wherever
we were going, and our pocket chatters.
The telephone has a mechanical voice

it works all day; it screeches, it turns,
it propels, it moves along so quickly
that I catch it like the clouds in front
of the moon, when it is bright and full.
Complaining serves no one, and suppose
I did find position, suppose I did find
worth outside of chronicling the damned war
and telling about the fickleness of words?

Word Star

I want to tell you that I love you
like I've never loved anyone before
of course my love list is long
and is full of catastrophe. But let's
not mourn the fallen roses in winter
or the way the sun retires without dread.
Let's not be sad. I know nothing
that grief can give; it is an empty vessel
and before long we'll forget
that there was goodness not ephemeral
not like a feather swaying through air
on a lost day. It's time really. That is
the message, that is the mission essential
that everything is today, now time.
Tears are yesterday's passion and today
is full of goodwill, tender thoughts

and soft ripe wishes under the streams
of river stars dancing stepping out
in the glowing evening restoration
is at hand the gruff with well worn
fingers at a machine for over twenty years
and today is my favorite and my charity
extends throughout noisy pounding rooms
or eight hours at the combine shop
when there are five years to retirement
and the heart leaps at only rest. I love
you when people want their rights
and the country is led astray
and all patriots feel it's too late to
make it right, the way the left arm
swings the hammer or stick. I love
you in the most simple manner
on the brightest day glowing
or the darkest minute in old life.
Private sentiment is fine; no one
can talk of war or guns or clothes
hiding flesh from enemies. The world
is full of enemies, people who don't
like each other when driving very
fast past country white faces
with advertising of a tobacco product
on a sliding door. I still love you

and try to connect the elements
the lines the dots the faraway emotions
that come to me when O poetry
captures my bird in the fist tight
and unaware, not knowing, never
knowing swindling words or spiral
staircases. Now should I explain
what never can be told? Please
don't question my words now
after I've told you about my heart
and please don't wonder about
the value of poetry when we are so
far away. I croon a little
and will not discuss world affairs.
I've my 24-7 obsessions with time
and how long it's been
and long it will take to erase bad luck
when the mechanical phone rings
from out of area, that green space
home addressing nice letters
and pretty greetings, my sister, and
when many several doors close does the house
burst open like a firecracker, unravel
because people in power know too much
and today, today, an important court case
was adamantly considered unconstitutional

and the deep red dahlias bloom and fade
according to the six month summer swelter
today not feeble impotent yesterday
was abundant in sunshine and no sign
of slow steady rain in puddles wet socks
and they say I am better at this expression
than any pedagogical fiction is a lie
and how many lies have I told
so the brass-handled door wouldn't slam
and the rattling mice wouldn't creep
around dusty dirt musty hard covers
in white bookcases on white walls?
I constantly wait. I dream. I suppose
many high-minded ideas in thoughtless
actions busy with children chores
and appointments. I could not
impress the gatekeepers; they sensed
my hesitation and noted my worry
when the myrtles bloom late
and the lighted slant of September rays
kiss the ground above leaves drying
my eyes commotion my interstate in sight
on the way home to the river's brown
might and conclusion. I'm alive
and weary.

Nature battles all; it duals and fights
back it will not go to sleep with harsh
words so it often speaks of peace
the way the snow arranges itself
on mountains when the crystal is blue
and red and blue drawing sight
into focus and I showed off my peculiar
steps in my starched creased striped blouse
for I had no suit, so silk scarf, no pin
or heels.

The position came and left me in loss
it is the greatest fight letting the poplar
leaves fall. The battle is not a war
in the usual sense; the bombs do not fall
but it must be endured like the heat
and it will wane although wishful thinking
and optimism stop by my house
and seldom stay. I promised you a better
story and there is one if you look into my purse
with the white soothing cream for skin aliments.
Why should I speak so hackneyed so trivial
when I'm trying to explain the exact nature
of yellow tired leaves making off from the stem?
It is a perilous escape and deer free of the hunters
when wind whooshes through gutters

eaves, and a country dog's scant fur becomes thick.
I will have no regrets and will smile
and end this obsession about occupation.
I turned it down. The world is occupied
and cannot be bothered; statesmen make off
with the bandit's booty being stellar
and principled. Principle will confuse
you and every refusal can be about a lofty
order, the conscience of kings and public
servants who dine on gold-trimmed plates
bestowing honor on loyal mediocrity
on simple fellows who like to gab. I love
it because the company is fine, and the
hours speed with peppery wheels over
desert roads where the heat radiates
like fumes; the desire is the problem
and now it is September, who can say
when the weather will turn teasingly cool
when the engine is hot and black suited
men still preside over fabulous meals
with straight crisp white shirts decorated
with fire engine roses wilting no more.
This is the perfect story I've told you
about and were you listening
as deaf conductors who remember yesterday
with an ear's memory? Do you care

about lost hunting seasons when the deer
runs away from predators and armed
men and women with full grocery sacks
come upon the scene, and there are hearty
feasts when the cooks work in stainless kitchens?
Nature can tell you, call and wait upon
your sterling guests with loose dollars,
a beauty queen's ransom. Kings and queens
do matter here losing no authority on
account of dining officials who bet
on the fawn's fate in cushioned forests.
Blame it on September, the quick way
that walkers move when a chill waits
for its day. I call this poetry, the mix
of words in patterns unknowing
and unknown to onlookers with glances
over surfaces like countertops
and the level of shining liquid in tumblers
or house ware glasses in sets, coming in
a pack of eight. I term this poetry, the word
dances through parades, digs for meaning
when it eludes the smartest brilliant
people.

I truly did not asked you to come here
and see how the sky clears and Pluto
is left abandoned by scientific engineers
who seldom chat with quarrelsome neighbors
over overgrown weeds in the neat nearby lawn.
Why do I talk about chatty men and celestial
bodies in half sentences making exacting
professors wince? You came here on your own
so don't accuse me of being obscure.
I learned verse around a table and sought out
praise from divas and egotists. Are you surprised
that I would tell you that, you whom I barely
know, who comes to my poetry with rules.
I broke the rules of poetry while bearded bards
were watching and yet none cried out thinking
it not worth a tirade, a diatribe, a rebuke. Blame
hesitant September or a month that pleases
you but is of no matter. The rebel knows
his cause and what must be done when food
covers every inch of a dining room table.
Nature will not deceive you and you'll know
who you are after the revolution if you decide
to participate, but do not accuse my verse
for it is honest.

The world finds its verity in newspapers
with happenings in faraway places.
I look for it in texts and imagine
that well-considered words contain
what I shall never know beyond my bleating.
So are you distant from me now, because
you wanted too much that I could not give?
Distance senses its place and never stops
from trying to separate us. I wouldn't lend
it a dime for identifying space. People
write to me from out-of state, and I answer
their letters quickly, much in the same manner
that lightening strikes, zigzagging in trucks
across West Virginia mountains, the turns
will amaze you, and I'll try to tell you
a folktale of no importance other
than someone spoke it before. I like stories
that are passed down from others
even though they have confused me
for I've thought they were true
and not entertainments. Do you know
or have I told you that most tales are meant
to wholly delight; bliss isn't correct
to the seriously downtrodden. The stories
can't be easily told, and we can revel
in hard facts like the stone of a courthouse

or of a gray statue in the empty square.
I talk very big for some who knows
little about a stranger's plight.
You are the one I've always known
and are no more familiar than New York
or the bustle, the taxi drivers, the food
venders. You are the invited
and the one who sees bars on the doors
keeping out feeling like the light switch
ushering in square dark places
where I might stumble
banging into walls black with the night
new in the day and manageable. How
do you love me now, who can only love
barely with a dull pain in my side
changing my usual awkward gait
for fear of pulling muscle
pounding like my restless heart
with no takers? And now I give
you my stories, the forgotten ones
in dreams that go like past reality
but what is that really, a truth for today
when the voices clamor and excite
in vindication and assuredness
of a certain but concrete moment
when elements come together

leaving one alone like the house
on a quiet morning on an uncomfortable
couch with the dog sleeping in a forbidden
chair.

Could you take me or leave me?
Indifference steals, creeps into
our affair, and I knew you wouldn't stay
long once you heard about other's tales
with saliva harmonicas and folk guitars
low melodies, off-beat strumming ballads
home or studio recordings the way you move
when the sweet sway hits the autumn trees
when they have gloriously lost their green,
thank goodness that eventually
they lose that monotonous color.

Ice Castle

I will build an ice castle
with gables porches
circular foyers
long carved stairways
to slick foreign tile
seal the windows
the doors with water
from a garden hose
better for roses
it is a bitter prison
that will melt
before the masses
the cheering audiences
in balcony seats
cell tight closed solid
situated in air
in the Southern sun
now its openings shine
flow into streams
like the rushing
of a springtime river
on a strong hiker's way
a steady gait firm
brown cedars
asleep from the season
before flowering trees
make dogwood hoes
the crooked handles
and the night is over
it does not hold anyone
its shrinking locks break
with glittering warmth
ardent fiery yearning
at last finally to be free.

When I Return

If I could remember
my whole life
and put it in front
of me like a road
through Kentucky
where the cedars
grow marching
along the blacktop
in communities
in the shade
of the sycamores
white patchy
memories come
and they go
they are happiness

after the sun
goes down
behind the trees
and the water is clear
always familiar
it is the same
when I return
in stump coves
in a song
or written word
see the pieces
what I can put together
after time dulls
wise certain sayings.

Churchgoers

Language of the heart
compassion discernment
the dark night of the soul
words church people use
they are kind enough
but never know
how to say, "no."
These people haunt me
shadows step close
stand next to me
monk silences meditation
singing songs chants
for everyday goers
who work for the homeless
in urban headquarters
some watch children
after years of politics
scholars graduates
I feel let down
no promised holiness
no prophets or saints
Why should I care
about motivation
question credibility?
The steeple can be seen
from the East and West
from the street sermons
eloquent
and intelligent. I will
not be Thomas
who needed to witness
proof to believe.

Blowing Rock

The breeze felt
like birth
exactly freeing
the body
from heat
wetness
that could go
on forever.
Strollers
pass with infants
safe and secure
tied into movement
the wheels
hopping
over steppingstones
The old couple
sit on the park
bench waiting
for a new scene
they are onlookers
and the world
is a sight
of children
on shoulders
and people on
their way
to art fairs
down slanted roads
to silver jewelry
and photographs
of barnyards
and snowy landscapes
too unbelievable
for summer
where mountain
men sell apples
at roadside stands
the turning road
going home.

Helen

She irons clothes
and welcomes
her daughters to church
where the family
sits in the same pew
I've known her
for years
and she is comfortable
with card games
and coffee
in the morning
with friends who chat
about bedspreads
and curtains
who make small talk
and go to Sunday
school. I think
she is sincere
and does not care
who wins elections
life is simple
life is holy
life is done right
when the offspring
brings the salad
and the husband
is away from home.

Prediction

I will come apart
like an old shirt
soft warm checkered
sophisticated flannel
elbows wear thin
two bony points break
through the seasons
winter collar frays
at its natural crease
there is a hole
under the arm.
A button comes off
then another
two sides fly in the wind
separating flapping
the torso exposed
the sleeves shrink
from the dryer
and go around
with electric socks
eventually I become
squares for dusting
fine slick furniture
high oak woodwork
that darkens the room
making it sober
even with white paint
call it destiny
the way material things
are supposed to go
no secondhand use
or a sad trip to charity.
I will be given another
chance transformed
into cleaning rags.

Easter 2009

Tongues of flames
on mountaintops
the maples upward
the eye follows
the day into Easter
red buds growing
from rock cuts
along highways
the image changes
into a holy face
when I was lost
between interstates
sign problems
of going anywhere
across borders
plowed fields
the people I love
delivered in dreams
the mind solves
its own island maze
and settles for rest.

Omen

Sooner or later
you will know
what will kill you
the cough
the leg limp
the extraordinary
pain grief
and it will not scare
you because
you've seen it
for years.
It has chased
you in the dark
until the day
the clear vision
of freedom running
from the tremor
from the ache
prescription
glass in the junk
pile before
you wondered
about mortality
and the people
who care
about you
the long scar
stretching across
the abdomen
and you will
see it after surgery
the thing
that will do you
in put you
in the grave
the telling years
you know them
well tough rugged
ending.

Process

The going back and forth
the limbs move carrying
the directions for the
machine
with the wheels rolling
and the plastic gears
of a child's contraption
or toy that goes from here
to there. The sun touches
the horizon line and tells
of morning until the scene
is old, the words older
and yet it watches the earth
and its mechanical trip
around recipes tucked into
boxes on the counter
or stored in a red and white
book above the stove.
The stand up mixer whirs
without batter, it takes
the steel around, its sounds
awaken
coffee drinkers on the way
down the steps to the smell
of work, spent old, dirty rags
trying to make something
into a product that can be
packed
into crates, shipped over
rivers,
driven to markets, minted
coins drop into registers
and feel cold in pockets.
I wanted it done,
so I ask you for a ride past
traffic wondering how to get
from here to there without
taking the steering wheel
to drive. *

*Previously published in the Hollins Critic
Vol.46 No.3 June 2009

Millennium

Afflicted hearts pulsing back blood
to the brain
and eyes. Make sense
of what you see here,
of gangster meanness
the gait attached
to swinging fists. Look
for yours, hear it
its strained resolve for remedies, leaves
and potions. Disembodied
organ, memory
of Rose of Sharon, planted
too closely to a chain-linked
fence, past all borders,
it beats still.

My mother tells me that she can't talk,
her hands are swollen
and I say that I am sorry
for the pinched nerve
that causes her pain,

my news, the connection I want
to make says, "I'll keep in touch."

I see in the grocery store,
on magazine racks, black
and white print. I see celebrities
and they say you are coming
for a second time. You will see
the heap that I speak
of and know the hearts again
that drove you home. I
tell you that they cry in their sleep
and take out the trash
on Monday.

II.

I imagine, sometimes
that you'll come to Denver first.
Your figure, your outstretched arms, sturdy
as a medal
will stop I-70 motorists. Twenty years ago
the lighted cross scared
me, the glare
from the mountain, shining
into my eyes
and down on a deep ascending road.

I learned to drive past accidents there
and how to make love in an apartment
above the Ace High Tap
to drink a case of beer between Golden
and Central City with Iowa friends,
we all knew that this was flight, the beginnings
of thinking that the soul
could be moved, uprooted,
and set down again,
the new ground replaced the past. There were new
skis for my birthday and unknown roommates
who drank shots and spoke of paying the "wooder" bill
the East was in the West.

I have looked for the place
without suffering.
Remembering resorts coins
of autumn aspen,
the history came back,
a grandmother
who stuffed baubles
in her chest of drawers, filling
them with a hundred losing sweepstakes tickets
a score of watches replacing
the one that her mother broke
on graduation day,

lonely records of dinners, dates,
the clothes were from her daughter's wedding
the father was too drunk
to walk down the aisle.

My mother made love to a black suit,
it wasn't blue
It was black shoes, tie
and trousers, the shoes were heavy
like concrete
and walked like jackhammers
across carpet, there was a pattern
on the toes
thick darkness to the heel.
It owned the utilities, the light switches
and newspapers rolled into fire
in my hearth home,
in my home hearth.
It was no banker, Diane.

That stalker, history. I married the son
of the superintendent of schools, a childhood prince
with manners and knew good people, people
who never crossed
a picket line or freed
a captive, goodness that render no justice

to the innocent caught
up in politics. Consensus
was not always kind. In practical living rooms,
looking for the place without pain,
the healers wore flat shoes
and chanted:
This house with its marble tile
and cherry finishes
will come down hard on disbelievers
and let me say no to Mrs. Waterbucket
when she calls to save the groundwater
or the groundswell
of public opinion on favored officials.
It will make my children Congressional scholars
and sweet music will flow from their fingers
and leave no smudges on my grand.
If I want I can hide my husband's mistress
in a walk-in
and he'll become the envy of every girl
who ever called a lawn care service.
His teeth will become orthodontically correct
and friends will imagine that he's big
on exotic vacations. This is my house. We built
it. It speaks for itself. It speaks foreign languages.
It speaks well.

III.
Lady Silence sits in leather interiors, driving past museums and galleries. It is just as well. She cannot buy expression.

But once a musician played a flute below her hill
And she listened for a while, even walked down a slope.

His wild hair frightened her; he couldn't be taken out.
Still for a moment, he wished that he's stay in her world.

But such are dreams, and the best people have them. He didn't stay. Before, he left Lady Silence took his instrument.

She keeps it in a firebox with crickets and sobs. All her commitments are there, a last "I love you," dated somewhere around 1962.

IV.
The air is absurd after music
so empty that three whistling birds
cannot fill the space. Pray for hot
tires and quick stops, the taxi door
slam, the hiss of wet streets
after rain when the pelting like
a heart beats, the night's pulse
from purple black clouds, unrelenting.

V.

Magnificent healer, most gentle of men, crimson leaf of new birth, what horse-nosed
petal grows among thorns? I know that expression is Grace, the word resounds, is heard
even in delicate whispers, the beauty rose, a once waxed stem can thunder and split the sky.

Iris

Cut while in bloom,
you were an iris in middle pinks
and purples, mauve.
No one could see your fluid run
into the vase only
your soft petals, ornate fading
growing dark.

I watched you wither while
the world marveled at your hues.
How much more beautiful
could you become
until you became nothing swept
off the table until another spring?

The Raft

In my dreams
I am a swimmer stretched
out across the water
slightly bowed
a feather's spine
reaching for a raft
and I see you
and want to save
you and other people
as well. It is sad
that they were set adrift
on a wooden raft.
I reached for you
and the makeshift boat
pushed away teasingly
like in a love story
where things
don't work out
as planned; somebody
is left crying
wailing about fairness
and how sweetness
should reap the same.
I swam to you
pulled through the water
its transparent blue
and you moved
up to the very front
on the tilted board knowing
I couldn't catch
you like a high ball
in a summer dirt field
or a lucky fish
on its way back home
behind the rocks.
I don't know
if you laughed
because it is funny
how dreamers
imagine perfect endings
in deepest sleep.

Lucky Star

It is hard to tell
if the stars shine on me
locating breath
and I might be
in the right place
after wandering
between genres
and churches
doctrines and creeds.
I might be dressed
for the party
a welcomed guest
sweet and visited.
Roll from my fingers
hopeful passion
heaven's fine light
give me a home
in kind neighborhoods
under settled skies.

Fans

Ceiling fans turn
tiredly above our heads
time's movement
around years
the graying
the repose
of motion
after eyes
catch each blade
and stop
the circular dances
are exhausted still.

Mean Dog

A retriever stands
in the side street
repaired with tar
walking toward
a moving car.
It has seen meaner dogs
or known confinement
on a chain in the backyard
the pulling has made
it free. It is unafraid.
The car swerves
finally moves out
of the way. What nerve
to stand in front of steel
and pretend invincibility
we should be more like
that not quivering
when danger comes
to us in its varied forms.
Toughness is a virtue
in an uncertain world
where bombs go off
and fathers don't pay
support the body grows old
maybe the dog could not
see or hear
and there is something brave
about that as well.

Tourist

I hope that I'll never
be a tourist
and want to roam
ancient alleys
to cathedrals
ruby enshrined rooms
to read foreign menus
and drink local brew
a strong Christian wine
I will stay home
and complain about
the heat never finding
myself in a land
tediously unknown.
Moving drains and makes me
long
for the past. I have spent
much time
in yesterday
where cities are kinder
and buildings
were beside the river
and a two-steeple
church could
be seen from the road
with orange cones
and reflecting barriers.
I have been places that
I should have never
left and so do not want
quaint cottages
or romantic rides
down celebrated streams.

Bright Air

Finally the open door
bright air
the bricks fall
the concrete exposes
bent steel rods
that have kept me
so unheard.
I have been yelling for
decades
inside thick walls
Now I step out.
amazed at freedom
there is the unbelievable
the impossible
stacked straw
sweaty livestock
nature's mute feeling
inarticulate life
The outside knows me

My words are faint.
I remind them
and they recall the fetters, cut
skin,
bruised bones
from trying to walk
on a straight path.
I am through the passage
my gait is steady
and shoes sound
one after another.
I move forward
without barricades
to be arriving at anticipated
places
the lifted voice
talks announces sings
about confinement's end.

Backwards

Rabbits lucky
feet line the road
like they are waiting
for a parade.
The thing
that holds out
is the reason
why so many
creatures stand
in morning
slight water sitting
expecting
or content
with the new day.
When we wait
time goes
so slowly
that it might go
backwards
making its way
into the past.
Rabbits are
in grass behind
bushes tucked
into gardens
before they come
to see each other
in crooked rows
they must greet
and appreciate
their kind
and onlookers
are the ones that
think dreams
will materialize.

Exchange

The flowers aren't silk
but they are fake
like plastic fruit
with real flaws
the apples and oranges
the grapes
disapproving mothers
toward suitors
flattering words
but a false exchange
they fool visitors
confound them
which was not their
initial function.
I wanted beauty
arranged fiction
to last to stay in place
and never to change
the lilies with no smell
neither of freshness
no age. Their stems
are unbelievably straight
reach upward
at the room's center
to the right height
short people can see
across them talk
to each other
without leaning too much
and their petals
exist perfectly
in space. They
can never leave
or find the end
of their journey
across time. Yet
they do not cry
or fuss. They
are contained
in a gray vase
and can only stand
still being decoration.

Dietrich

Do you ever tire of the silence?
Does it move you to books?
The story of a man in prison
in dark uncertain times
with prayers for his release
letters are to his parents
and to dear friends who know
his fate better than grocery lists
or mundane common chores
Do you ever look down on poetry
for what it cannot achieve?
It cannot ride horses making
quick getaways from persecution.
It has no real agency
beyond the response
of the heart not beating cruel
regimes with verbs. I believe
in words, and that is my joy
and also my sorrow
attempting to make them stick
so others can move freely
so that the mind can open
a steel grinding movement
then liquid reaches the surface
there is promise again.
Cutting metal is an exact
art and requires the worker
to wear gloves in case of accidents.
I know there will be
misunderstanding
people who ignore insights
who dismiss knowledge
fancy lies to decipher
the man in prison shuns

fearfulness wanting bravery more than pity. He is like us in his imposed confinement when captors are not kind and real action is out. We turn the pages to see what happens to the chained hero on paper, in another time.

Cloud Watch

I watched clouds,
played a child's
game saying what
they resembled until
high moisture
became the same
mass common concern
with no variation
and I wonder
if that is what it
is to grow old
acquainted with
the above
the heavens
where jets streak
and birds rise
from marshes
in a Southern
land near the sea.
The single figure
the only one
that might nourish
and give energy
but it cannot
be separated
cannot be its own
now when the car
drives fast down
the interstate
other cars passing
never knowing
how the prospect fails,
is limited
with the attempt
to name.

Loss

I think of losing you
and the world
does not seem right
or fair or just
or able to relax
after ten hour days
when the feet swell
and the waves
leave the center
of the ocean
they leave
all they've known
to come to shore
where swimmers
stroke the birds
peck at the sand
looking for morsels
and then dropping
one that the surf
steals with its force
the foam coming
and going
in front of a house
with a palm tree
near the drive. I
lament the passing
of time crying
a little more
at small thoughts.

Stations of the Cross

"Pilate…brought Jesus outside and took a seat on the judge's bench…He said to the Jews, 'Look at your King!' At this they shouted…Crucify Him!' In the end, Pilate handed Jesus over to be crucified."

(John 19:13-16)

Jesus Is Sentenced to Death

I am the witness
of things not right
a woman
in an earth-rocking crowd
colliding elbows
clashing breath
indecipherable noise
Today, sometime
in the future
I watch
and listen
waiting for history
to retell
an ancient story.
Men are elected
they post signs
and run ads
while the rains
flood Texas
It would happen again

the bloodlust
never ended
with thousands
of years
of knowing
the ordained
stand in front
of congregations
the man
the woman
who went to a seminary
who wrote papers
on God
to tell quaint stories
little life lessons
in sermons
in homilies
people pleasers
a little joke
to laugh
before seriousness.
What have we learned
in pews? What
have we picked up
from textbooks?
The world is not
at peace
and a holy
man calls for mercy
the truth is threatened
or erased
the facts denied
we make plans
for what is believed
to be a better place
men of ideas
these political suits
colorful ties
silk pockets
campaign slogans
aimed at winning
it thunders in January
and the locals predict
snow white stuff
within seven days.

It's man-made
climate change
extreme weather
another record
month. I stand where
folks have gathered

for a rally or a trial
Who is innocent
these days? We
have not learned even
while we have
the Scripture
we can recite it
like the alphabet
or prayers
a pledge of allegiance
possibly to sinister men
who no longer pretend
to offer light
their candles'
flames dimly sway
and we stumble
in darkness
in an unhappy gait.
2015 was the hottest year
so go to the beach
in bathing suits
in fashionable bikinis
to rest in the sand
or climb
on granite rocks
where fishermen cast lines
in the rising surf
some ride waves
with gulls around
the ocean is rolling
constant
a slight breeze
the visit complete.

The official's voice
serves interests
pacifying a mob
saying Jesus must die
crucify him
all aren't here
some are in dwellings
on the mountain
or past a blooming field
shaking their heads
in disapproval
the proverbial disapprovers
that done, they go
about business
go to important forums
sit in meetings
chatter in lobbies
they meet Pilate's

decree with silence.
They feel wronged
but go home
to dinners
to public events
where children study
are taught
spelling reading
arithmetic
adding 2+ 2
the people say
they can do nothing.
They can not change
the direction
of the morning sun
beating down
moving from chair
to chair as it rises
waves cannot be altered
they roll forward
and back; the outcome
the sentence
does not change
with wishful thinking
or faint prayers
acceptance is key

dissent is a matter
for the unconnected
for those who live
in the margins
for activists
with nothing
to lose
with light sleep
and the wind blows
rain at the openings
of nooks
and crannies
all day and night
sealed from elements.

The crowd is satisfied
mostly thinking
the happenings are just
the innocent's fortune
is part of the day's news.
How cheap life
has become today
after history, yesterday
when a man healed the sick
raised the dead
and walked on water

experience does not save
the rejected one
who was not interviewed
to be the Savior
of the world.
The story is told
for generations
in pew learning
steadfast followers
who deny the ocean rising
the sun melts
ice sheets

the permafrost
skiers move to other slopes
the man is chosen
for death while
the azaleas bloom
in red, pink, and white,
along a winding road
in a hog automobile
that barely
fits in one lane.

"If a man wishes to come after me, he must deny his very self, take up his cross and follow in my steps. Whoever would preserve his life, will lose it, but whoever loses his life for my sake and the gospel's will preserve it."

(Mark 8:34-35)

Jesus Carries His Cross

The sharp heavy angle cuts
into his shoulder.
This is the fulfillment
of prophecy
that one carries
the weight
of the angry world
people who sleep
in the open
on park benches
while billionaires
are tucked
into bed sheets
others' hunger
prompts stealing
for food
sustenance
the rejection

of the miserable
where poverty
is a crime. No crime
was committed
the mind is focused
on the bruising beam
that wears
into flesh see
obedience
the God
submits to be human
vulnerable
like soft arms
that carries earthen jars
of murky water
and bread
for the children
who do not see
mean spectacles
the structure drags
the flesh bleeds
the sky is gray
with the threat
of rain. The innocent
wonders, aware
in the moment

chaotic voices are heard
all around him. He
thinks he hears
his mother, then
the testosterone commands
of soldiers go in
and out of consciousness
he feels the burden
like he were an animal
with a cruel yoke
laughter intrudes.

The rain pours
throughout the night
on Christmas Eve
in a Southern hub
with nonstop flights
to anywhere
record rainfall
the rivers swell
water travels swiftly
it overflows
its muddy banks
sending water into interiors
the cell phone alarm sounds
flash flood watch

Concerned people talk
about justice
neighbors come out
to see the aftermath
of violence blood
on the ground
from a shooting, folks
looking for answers
looking for community
where citizens gather
everybody says it's too bad
that young people
die, are cut down
in this year of mercy
a holy man prays
asks that others pray
for him. The weight
of the world
is on our God,
he trudges, hearing
that it seems unfair
and someone asks
who is responsible
no one like the quiet
streets, like the house
in the middle
of the subdivision
on a full-mooned night.
This is what happens
when love is abused
red broken bricks
on a downtown street
porous blocks
the white cement
of torture go along
the picture window
the emergency room
where beds roll past
the Savior must
have thought
about prior acts
of believers
of going into common houses
of driving
out demons
simple conversations
with friends, the 12
who watched miracles
were at the baptism
when the Father
sent the Spirit
from heaven

He was pleased
as perspiration rolls
down Jesus' neck.
It is holy water.

In a moment of awareness
Jesus hears a bird sing
nature would seem
to conspire, there is one
that does not. There
is a soft sound
a fluttering take-off
feathers in motion
his lungs heave out air
resolve takes over
in his mind
choices are gone
he must fulfill
go through
with the divine plan.

The high point
across from a river
is where my body trembles
others decide
I am cold

covering my shoulders
fireworks explode
in the sky
colors against black
reflected on water
on a spring evening
music plays
an old time spiritual
swing low
everything is festive
between heaven
and hell the crowd
eats pizza slices
from a downtown vendor
with food trucks
a band of angels
looking after me
on the hill
this is the first time
that I felt his cross.

My Catholic grandmother
lived
on a bluff
with a thick line
of uncut grass

with tall seeds
and rising green
with spotted pears
on the ground
beside a highway
where the cars
went fast sounds
of rushing speed
between an embankment
and a pasture
on their way
to the county seat.
She talked
about carrying crosses
the burden
of a common life
when machine shop wages
only stretched
so far when
the husband drinks
and no longer drives

because of an accident
where one was killed.
She raised four children
in a small frame house
until vandals
painted her furniture
with fingernail polish.

Her father gave me
a plastic rosary
and I accepted it like a toy.
I did not then know
how to pray. It is the memory
of the man who also picked
wild blackberries
and carried
them in malt cups
and often stood
at the gravel-scraping
double doors
of a white shed

"But he was pierced for our offenses, crushed for our sins. Upon him was the chastisement that makes us whole, by his stripes, we were healed."

(Isaiah 53:5)

Jesus Falls for the First Time

The burden is too much
The following crowd is
convinced
it knows for certain
that the condemned
man is no God
now. Some whisper,
some taunt, feeling satisfied
about judgment weakness
makes people meaner
weakness emboldens
them they embrace
their crime
would vote
for the bully
the one who pushes
others around
and shoves
into positions
calls out opponents
The mob fights
for power

denies the journey
some would find
a champion
in overbearing
voices the rude banter
of onlookers
who worship strength
solid toughness
and would whip a dog.

There is no part
of the bruised bone
that does not sting
burn with weight. My Lord
falls,
is counted a failure.
He does not rise above
miserable circumstance
must have no connection
for most think
the blessed
have an easy road.
lean steaks hot soups
the best seats
in the warm house
only good theater

for public men
poll numbers rise
if we are able; there
will be no stumble or fall.

The cross is awkward
the sin too heavy
oil is cheap now
people don't care
about renewable energy.
Grimy fossil fuel
drives a warming world
suppresses the truth
a butterfly in December
designed paper-like wings
land on bushes
out of place
for the season
the missing bees
portend famine
bears walking
on thin ice. We cannot
concern ourselves
most citizens are fed
and satisfied.
Rain hits against

the window
it sounds all night
the now frequent deluge.

Pope Francis calls
for mercy assures us
that God forgives
wrongful deeds
over and over
a thousand times
because of love.

He never tires
of healing men

Jesus is the promise
if we repent
yet oil companies
are not sorry
for the Iraq War
for their part in history
Who will say
the prayers
of penance
for those who bomb
for a commodity
to make profits?

"This child is destined to be the downfall and rise of many in Israel, a sign that will be opposed and you yourself shall be pierced with a sword."

(Luke 2:34)

Jesus Meets His Mother

Mary knew the price
of the immaculate conception
A heart wholly human
breaks for her son
on his path
to a criminal's death
to execution.
Her obedience
is signature
she said yes
to bear a divine child
for God, but now
she prays to the Father
to call it off
Jesus meets his mother
She bore the world's wrong
that day every hunger
every addiction
every lack
a heart mirroring his
own the mother
sees pain

in his eyes
the mocking crown
the mean-spiritedness
of thorns piercing
his forehead.

Nature must weep
for her. The animals stay
close to their nests
they do not venture far
from their young.
Their pity is silence
they do not cry
They have no sound today.

Jesus meets a steady love
like when the electric door
is closed coffee comes
in disposable cups
people gather
in a smoke-filled room
the blue cloud chokes
conversations
meant to pass
the time
a roommate sings in French
then English
about red roses
has a boyfriend
named Harley
or Charlie
the windows are covered
with wire mesh. Sweet
mother's face who
crochets plum-colored throws
for wing chairs
records chicken pox
measles, mumps
in the family Bible
who types letters
to the apartment
with a view
of the foothills.
The wild dream is over.

The sky is heavy purple
cars approach travel
into the coming rain.
The old trees lining
the tobacco town road
are bulging
at the base

are deformed
little branches sway
are blown off
like failed kites
twigs and leaves litter the
streets
then the blinding rain.

Mary thinks of childbirth
remember hours
of labor
the pushing
until finally
the infant rests
on her stomach
the beginning
of caring deeply
of worry
of knowing his life
must be extraordinary
his words must be written
down he moves people
to sacrifice luxurious
lifestyles
the comforts riches
I am the woman artist
who witnesses
who bleeds
who attests
who creates
like her
so that humanity
can go on
the baby's wet head
short scarlet limbs
belong to the world's Savior.

I sing with my mother's
voice, rich, deep penetration
that cries beyond
our space, beyond our time
into the past.

Jesus saw his mother,
and went on.

"As they led him away, they laid hold of one Simon the Cyrenean who was coming from the fields. They put a crossbeam on Simon's shoulder for him to carry along Jesus."

(Luke 23:26)

Simon Helps Jesus Carry His Cross

My eye now catches
a worker coming
in from a neighboring field
He looks strong,
able to lift the weight
for a line of soldiers
leading Jesus
to his death.
The soldier commands
the passing stranger
to help Jesus,
the targeted politico
the man who rocked
the little boat
who did not go along
with authority
who is counted
as a criminal
Simon is unsure
but he is subject
to enforcers
lifts the cross

is now complicit
with the angry crowd.
The laborer thought
that he had no choice
like citizens
the people
who disagree
with policies
of tyrants
and demagogues
or who would accept
immigrants
who are to be returned
to war-torn countries
lost safety
of thousands denied
and overlooked.
The newcomer

is despised
and unwelcomed
the worn script
has been known
the past
is recited.
I am not telling
any breaking news
no stunning headline
the water floods
the streets swirls
with jutting debris
from former patios
the destruction
of obstacle homes
the pot-hole softness
of broken saturated roads.

"A great crowd of people followed him, including women who beat their breasts and lamented over him."

(Luke 23:27)

Veronica Wipes the Face of Jesus

A woman feels compassion
and removes her veil
She, moved by the sight
of suffering, seeks
to soothe
the struggling man.
Veronica wipes his face
from toil burden
the road dirt
dust rising
from a dragged cross
dried and wet blood
from injury. Does she sense
that this prisoner
on his way
to excruciating death
is the Christ
who fulfills prophecy
and gives his life
for an unworthy crowd?
How undeserving
we are common

people fathers
mothers brothers
and sisters
who can watch injustice
beckoning
it on. Indifference
is the worst wrong scenes
of a painful circumstance
and we are numb
or hiding out
from daily news
of shootings
in small paragraphs
on the back pages
of newspapers
we are busy
hard unmoved
but in the procession one
goes forward
a story recorded
passed down
on account
of a gesture
of kindness

that is taught
in religion classes
the named woman in history.

The rain taps
against windows.
It comes down for hours
without pause
a car swooshes past
a cloth hanging
from the passenger side
wash it clean remove
meteorologists reports
of extreme weather.
The Scripture
is not unknown to us,
the end
of denial is near
when pretending
falsehood
is ripped away
the man staggers
and there is an imprint
of his face

of the redeemer
on fabric
I am only a witness
in wee hours

when the world sleeps.
I turn on the porch light
to see the evening
it spotlights blown rain.

"Your attitude must be that of Christ…
Though he was in the form a God, he did not
deem equality with God something to be grasp
at
Rather he emptied himself and took the form
of a slave, being born in the likeness of men.
He was known to be of human estate, and it
was thus that he humbled himself, obediently
accepting even death, death on a cross."

(Phil. 2:5-8)

Jesus Falls for the Second Time

Three soldiers gather
near the fallen man.
They confer wonder
why anyone
would mistake
the weakling
for a God.
They order
say that he must begin
again. They hoist
the cross
onto his small figure

not sturdy
like the legs
that cannot stand
the afflicted drops
to the carpeted floor
calling the name
of a loved one
one spring day
in an Asheville mansion.
The party tours
the grounds
appreciate gardens
tastes wine
from sampling cups.

It is coral calcium
strawberry pie
a fast ride down
the turnpike
firm destiny
in the making nature
is free along a river town
where water turned
the mill's wheel
and fermented brew

belonged to not quite
gangsters
but bosses
during prohibition
where stories
are told to children
who defend
their mothers
from thrown lamps
the black dirt
from a potted plant
on a wool rug. I am
the witness
of things not quite right.

The cross is placed
again the burden
the soldiers heckle
him he hears laughter
a low command
to pick up
the pace. He hears
the wooden cross cut
drag scrape
a groove
into the earth

and feels stinging
burning pain
on his shoulder.

He listens for his mother
in a blur of many voices
and craving
any sound
of sweetness, looking
for what
is familiar
his eyes follow his feet.
He cannot hear her now.

"Jesus turned to them and said: 'Daughters of Jerusalem, do not weep. Weep for yourselves and for your children."

(Luke 23:28)

Jesus Speaks to the Women of Jerusalem

Women walk beside
the broken gasping man
he turns his head
to see saddened faces.
He admonishes
the mournful witnesses
of his journey tells
the gathered
not to weep
do not cry for me
not to beat
their breasts
in protest. "Pray
for yourselves
and your children,"
he tells the women.

These are the women
of first histories
early records
who feel
for the injured

whose hearts
reach out
in compassion
to the innocent
to the abused
and wrongly condemned.
Christ's pain
did not escape
their senses
or eyes telling
all on the dark day
they were present
at the sham trial
following fate
of a gentle prisoner
a man who had healed lepers
and prayed
for the poor.

The circumstance
of women
yesterday, today
is from brutish lessons
on vulnerable flesh
famous strife
in paper books
primary sources
that tell
about battles coups
the whims
of violent men
who sit in legislatures
endlessly talking
about rights
of the unborn
while they beat
the world's girls
into submission
with edicts
and lawful decrees.

Oh women, take pity
heavy downpours
armed oppressors
the great mistakes
political decisions
church traditions
maddening hierarchies
that exclude
half populations
and rock
unsettle
silent generations
with sanctioned wrongs.

*"I am like water poured out;
all my bones are racked… my throat
is dried up like baked clay. My tongue
cleaves to my jaws; to the dust of death
you have brought me down."*

(Psalm 21:15-16)

Jesus Falls for a Third Time

His small body
is overwhelmed
cannot stand
his bleeding head
under lumber
red tinged curls
ringlets stiff
under crushing
weight weary eyes.
Soldiers curse
at the beaten life;
their job
is not easy. The man
should be tougher
on his way
to execution
he should have more fight
not collapse
they lift struggling flesh
to his feet

Now Time • 157

the knees sway
he trips forward
a little farther
up along the rising dirt path.
The following crowd
seems confused
for a second wonders
about the pathetic scene
Mary bears
her son's agony
his painful fail
she wants to go
to him but soldiers push
her back. God knows
his plan perfect
of divine obedience
resolve to complete
the journey
to a foretold end.
Prophets describe
the passion
in stories
and the rain comes
down in another city
in another time
after salvation

when people plead ignorant
about the toll
that has not been hidden.

Everyone professes
that love
conquers angry
men jealous
of rivals
kick-in ribs
break ankles
with black boots
or whatever footwear
the local villain
wears sports memories
in night dreams
waking the mind
to yesterday.

I read news articles
I am the witness
of corporate greed
that hides truth
with quack scientists
who pollute oceans
roast the air

where pelicans fly
in the morning looking
for schools. I see
the electronic ballot
switch votes
and know
a poll tax
on God-given rights.
I hear the rain blow
swirling waves
against glass.

My mother reads
about Fatima
the children's vision
she dwells
on the seals. What
can it mean
for a world in turmoil?
The woman
a New Windsor prom queen
with lifelong
night dreams
of apocalyptic desolation. She
prays
that her family
will taken up
in the rapture
to snickers
and dismissal
and a politician wins
an election. The rain pours.
She is alone
with a television
in a mint-green bedroom
and a Christian
friend who cleans
her house
does laundry
and leaves money
for her birthday
on the kitchen table.

"We should not tear it. Let us throw dice to see who gets it." (The purpose of this was to have the Scripture fulfilled. "They divided my garments among them, for my clothing they cast lots")

(John 19:24)

Jesus is Stripped of His Garments

The uncovering
of a brutalized captive
the injury
from lashes
marked torn flesh
wine-colored wounds
everyone can see
the result
of hatred
the actions
of hot mindless crowds.
When the clothes
are taken,
it is revealed
yet only women
the mother sees
knows with her heart
the damage
of the damning mob
ugly disclosure

no holding back
no more hiding
the truth
of human cruelty.

Jesus knows his fate
he is the ransom
like when souls combined
into a concentration
of the sin felt
seen during services

in another time
all mischief contained
in the body
when music played
and the impact
was palpable
the shock real
electrifying sensation
in the basement
where choirs practiced
in the chapel.

"When they came to Skull Place, they crucified him there and the criminals as well…

(Luke 23:33-34

Jesus Is Nailed to the Cross

The breaking
of bone
sounds of hammers
one criminal
is to the left
another to the right.
Our Lord
is crucified
in front
of a following crowd.
Did anyone watch
the pain
and attempt
to free him? The
Christ said, "Forgive
them, for they not what
they're doing." A man
so tortured
let them off. He
did not blame
or cast a stone
not interested in who
was guilty
time goes by

and we now recognize
the story
etched in
the mythos
repeated
for centuries
in the best places
so professed
for countless generations
in cathedrals
in country churches
where people kneel
with sacred words
on raspberry lips.

The poet's imagination
is faulted
for retelling
the Scripture.
A long poem
cannot convey
sacred meanings.
I pray but do not
know or suffer
like Christ.
The poet
is a wordsmith
a truth-seeker
but only guesses
when conveying
the divine plan,
a plan for the ages
of eternal things
that never go out
with time. Yet the crowd's
anger is not gone.
They have not loved
the rising oceans
the pelican
on its spiral dive
or the chatty gull.

*"When noon came, darkness fell
on the whole countryside and lasted
until mid-afternoon. At that time,
Jesus cried in a loud voice… 'My God,
my God, why have you forsaken me?'"*

Jesus Dies on the Cross

Jesus thirsts for water.
is given vinegar
His senses feel little
are numb; he dreams
of green fields
in the springtime
he is aware of pain
in moments. He hears
the voices of women
of soldiers. Moisture builds
in the sky, the sky
becomes heavy violet
he labors to breathe
cannot take
in a full breath.
He is aware
of his mother's
presence he looks
down at the crowd.
Christ knows
that it is almost over
he struggles, draws

in air. Clouds hide
the sun. Jesus again
asks for water. He hears
rumbles of thunder
the people begin
to scatter going back
on the trail
to their homes
the rain washes
his face
in lines streaks

the sweat
the blood
from his forehead
dirt rolls away
in tiny streams
from his arms
"My God, My God
Why have you forsaken me?"
His head drops
to his chest. It is done.

"As it grew dark… Joseph from Arimathea arrived—a distinguished member of the Sanhedrin… Then having brought the linen shroud, Joseph brought him down.

(Mark 15:42-46)

Jesus is Taken Down from the Cross

A group brings the linen
to take Jesus' body
from the cross.
The crowd has left
they have other concerns
now the evening menu
they hear
from wise men
who cannot remember
the commotion
that will only
come back
in dreams, how the sky
turned lavender
then indigo how
the rain pounded
the earth until every blade
and petal
was bent over
crushed
from tears.
The great thirst

could not be quenched
the people stood
by deep wells
with dry dippers
water flooded
the streets
in another time,

water rising
into living rooms. Water
everywhere, covering
the towns, the market
making
them appear
as rivers and seas.

"They took Jesus' body and in accordance with Jewish custom bound it up in wrappings of cloth and perfumed oils. In the place where he was crucified there was a garden…they buried Jesus there…"

(John 19:40-42)

Jesus is Laid in the Tomb

The story is familiar
so we experience
no alarm
or shame
we are assured
of mercy
promised forgiveness
salvation
in three days

smokestacks cloud
the sky. Did Jesus die
for corporations
for the bottom-liners
for drillers
and spillers
that cover
the pelican
with a suffocating fluid

for those who want profit
more than sustained life
on the planet?

Lamb of God
who takes away
the sins
of the world
have mercy on us.

Lamb of God
who takes away
the sins
of the world
have mercy on us.

Lamb of God
who takes away

the sins
of the world
grant us peace.

Neighborhood deer
eat white roses
in the middle
of the night
they cut the tender buds
and I sigh
considering
a loss
of extraordinary beauty.
the bushes
are left
the flowers
will come again.

Index of Bible Verses for Now Time

John 19:13-16	131
Mark 8:34-35	136
Isaiah 53:5	141
Luke 2:34	144
Luke 23:26	147
Luke 23:27	149
Phil. 2:5-8	152
Luke 23:28	155
Psalm 21:15-16	157
John 19:24	160
Luke 23:33-34	162
Mark 15:42-46	166
John 19:40-42	168

The Mother Word

An Exploration of the Visual

The Chandelier

Sunlight warmth
on the skin
on a temple
light flickers
flashes
with rushing speed
and blinds
an eye
in moments
something peaceful
a settling inward
speckled white moisture
forms mountains
in the sky
not threatening
the weather
has passed
leaving its drops
on lawns
on the heads
of people
driving convertibles
the rugged jeep
with a manual
transmission
confounding
a new generation
who reach
for uncertain stories
of allegiance
to the flag
recited in elementary schools
with written-on
dusty chalkboards
the light comes
in through low rectangular
windows
with steel frames
with a view
of parking lots
and paths
to statues
of saints, martyrs
covered

for Good Friday
the bright air prompts
a trip to the river
to a shop
with a broken sidewalk
a door handle
with a place
for a thumb
to press open
to relics
wooden bookcases
with Life magazines
award-winning
photography
for a 60s audience
thick leather volumes
cases of jewelry
with stories
of anniversaries
a loving forgotten couple
displays
of pins worn
on the chests
of matronly aunts
floral designs
semi-precious stones
from estate sales
everything
the dead remember
on special occasions
the antique rosaries
said how
many prayers
on an anxious day
or when one felt
particularly close
to the Lord
the metal crucifix
is tarnished
there are tea cups
a few strays
from china cabinets
in Victorian homes
only blocks away
from an international port
where sailors
came buying gifts
for sweethearts
in the day
of glamour girls
from the store's ceiling
hangs a crystal chandelier

and a string
with a price tag
cut heavy glass
in three tiers
sparkling radiant
a treasure
preservation
of departed souls
the family pictures
with an unusually tall son
in suspenders
women
wearing wool sweaters
and long skirts
entertained suitors
under its light
the patriarch
read newspapers
in armchairs
while the dog
slept in corners
under a table
the illumination
was enough to see
aspects of living
cutting up
a whole chicken
for dinner
before the great wars
when water
was pumped
from the deep well
to the kitchen
and a white stove
with a see-through door
featured hot coal
burning above
the fixture
with its six candles
witnessed brothers
arm wrestling
the heirs
who were the prize
of the group
college bound
while sisters fussed
with yarn
and scissors
measuring material
for everyday dresses
In the morning
the sun's rays

project colors
on the walls
telling stories
when white light
is broken down
refracted
into spectra
they are details
the personalities
of history
culture
exposed
in narratives
poetry
fairy tales
for lazy
onlookers
who go fishing
in coastal waterways
and dine
in restaurants
with pictures
on the wall
of the local catch.

Red Scare

Russians interfered
in the presidential election
the list of aides grows
the people
are not happy
even though
they do not remember
Sacco and Vanzetti
worries about
foreigners
immigrants
or Dorothy Day's
leftist companions
who hid out
in shoddy houses
were subject
to raids
hearings shaking
up Hollywood
the lovers
of the downtrodden
the poor
who worked
in factories
in mechanical yards

taking lunches
in sturdy pails
while soup lines
of unemployed men circled
the busy blocks
of cities with high rises
far from stockyards
where animals
came in trucks
to a four-way stop sign
the hired men
were butchers
meat-cutters
who fed
their children bread
potatoes
boiled bones
into broth.
Every good journalist
wrote exposes
about labor conditions
and wealth
was pervasive
in a different part
of town sweet cream
dark coffees

afternoon evening
beef roasts
and gravy over
the entire plate
soft down pillows
never dreaming
of unfortunate others

Bedtime stories
the bad wolf
dresses as a grandma
the menaces
are hidden
like the thief
who is never caught
red handed
when the myrtles
branches blow
scarlet flowers bloom
too early
in the year
and the temperature climbs
the pavement
red hot
everyone
is skeptical

of Russia
another scare only
this time
those who lack
are ignored
The real threat
the caution sign
the warning
in bold letters
isn't Marxist
or some theory
to soothe
the masses
about a dingy existence
coal miners
want more holes
in the earth
tunnels lined
with underground lights
when the dust
becomes heavy
alarms go off
red is danger
the planet lets
us know
of peril

and we are required
to listen

An ill-considered apple
was glossy red
the forbidden fruit
in the garden
with cherries
rhubarb stalks
so attractive
to the eye.
Watch that color
its spirit its power
in red silk ties
politician's garb
highlighting tan skin
the ability
to bamboozle
to provoke
the bullfighter's taunt.

Cinderella's Orange

When a pumpkin
is transformed
into a carriage
the middle-class

magical hope
is that the young woman
would not suffer
cruelty anymore
a lottery winner
in a garden fruit
with wheels
and footmen
a comfortable ride
to the palace
reveals dreams
wishful thinking
the harsher reality
a downside
with no leniency
when men show
off jumpsuits
at authorities jails
petty theft
armed robbery
and worse
the orange
of imprisonment
of being charged
dissidents
political prisoners

revolutionaries
ardent activists
rebel pens
that tout
uneasy truths
brilliant boat-rockers
locked away
alienated
and lonesome
with public defenders
plea bargains
rushed work
the innocent
are in with the rest
who wait
for court dates

High visibility
the hunter's outfit
a man is no deer
in the field.
the orange
jacket tips off
other's with guns.
detour signs
cannot be denied

like reflector cones
in road construction.
a man guides
his pick-up truck
through obstacles
a buck hanging
out of the tailgate
construction workers
wear bright vests
so others can see them.
life preservers
tying in front
the bulkiness
rough straps
so rescued boaters
can be reached and taken
up from the water

A fiery ball
spreading orange
on the horizon line
at sunset
a glowing star
burning
more heat
world tension

rogue nations
the possibility
of thermo nuclear war
wildfires
from climate change
orange needles
dried forests
Pedrogao Grande
hellish flames
consuming houses
businesses
terrorism
ever-looming
as beach-goers retire
shaking
off sand
with open car doors
putting children
into automobiles
people look
to the West over
water marsh
grasses to see
the searching
ibis's beak

Yellow Gold

A ring signals commitment
between lovers
individuals
who met
on the Internet
they might stand
at the altar
with sacred
adornments
on its surface
a weighty treasure
a would-be
pirate's booty
from rascals
who sailed
the ocean
and took whatever
they wanted locked
crates
chests full
of ornate
drinking cups
crafted goblets
the chalice
coin stacks
depicting the king's
insignia
his official
reign beads
strung
into fashionable necklaces
candle holders
the world
plots
clamors
for gold
at what price?
The prospector
with a pouch
of dust
wants to buy supplies
hammers
and picks
People will be
are betrayed
for riches
profit-mongers
put bounties
on the heads
of the poor
who want

thrift store rolls
the rounded tops
of warm loaves
with butter
sweet spread
instead
of the new military
industrial complex
corporate avarice
the despot's
opulence
the flashy ways
of authoritarian
government
subsidized
oil companies
in budget priorities
where invisible
humanity
is not counted.
Geography
is featured
in yellow magazines
best known
for poignant
pictures

of Arctic melting
of famine
the plight
of indigenous tribes

Green Fields

A long road trip
going home
to the Midwest
past cornfields
soybeans
sweeping green
for miles pines
beside farmhouses
wind buffers
where children
grow, the world
is growing
sprouting
flowering
beautiful grasses
every leaf
in summer
delights
the eye
seeing steeples

the courthouses
the neighborhoods
tended yards
the Paris Agreement
where citizens
care about green
trees cooling
the planet
the breeze blowing
through
covered limbs
the child
reaches an age
when called
an adult
experience
is all
that is needed
to know
about politicians
and how dollars
affect policy
big money cash
that keeps lawmakers
from saving
the shiny river
from chemicals
surrounded
by poplars
and other vegetation
that sucks
the water
into life.
the people
need plants
bushes vines
weeds
the stately oak tree
in front
of landmark houses
that have
been there
for over
a 100 years
on the streets
stray clumps blades
in the cracks
of concrete
cyclists watch
for emerald glass
on the road
the shattered

premium
beer bottle
thrown
from a party
where a blanket
was placed
on the ground
in the park
land set aside
so citizens
can play
musicians tune
instruments
on bandstands
they compete
with the faraway noise
of mowers
people want
more green
summer relaxation
the feeling
on being
with nature
canopied woodlands
hidden life
tiny heartbeats
of squirrels
raccoons
munching deer herds
opossum
the birds
that sit on branches
singing
and flying
through the day

Mother Blue

A seaside gazebo
protection
against the sun
the ocean mirrors
the cloudless sky
showing
little separation
between
air and water
the mother
and the child.
the self
sexual identity
is not yet
formed

the two are one
in rhythm
in motion
the body protrudes
goes into workplaces
into grocery
stores nestles
into a queen-sized bed
the womb
covers all
flowing
like the blue planet
where people live
on seven continents
discovered
by explorers
adventure
sanctuary
seekers
who set off
in uncharted seas
in storms
when crews
were washed overboard
swimmers
for survival

for pleasure
in clubby pools
women athletes enter
roped race lanes
the freestyle
breaststroke
backstroke
butterfly
timed events
all the ways
to reach back
to beginnings
to amniotic fluids
to sustenance
to victory
blue ribbons
to awards
the enjoyment
is the surf
rolling forward
and back
movement
where pelicans
hover over
curled waves
the birds

are hungry
for mullet
small fish
glittery scales
while humans return
to cultural icons
Mother Mary
in an ample
draping gown
with a border
the whale
a mammal
that nurtures
her calf
in blue seas
and migrates
up the Eastern coast

Vineyard Violet

Philosophers
the mystics
the teachers
in book-lined rooms
in studies
in classrooms
at the academy
the imagination
the invention
is full of ideas
with a sketch
or a plan
speculation
about the view
from the top
of purple mountains
the height
the depth
the width
of the soul
in paintings
in essays
in poetry
when the bard
creates rhythms
with language
that comes
in dreams
the apparitions
the characters
who play a part
in night chatter
the half realities

when the mind
interacts
awakes
to its concerns
its desires
sleep patterns
its knowledge
of good
and evil collide
into what
can be discerned
remembering
scenes
absurdities
before consecrated wine
touches
the tongue
uplifting spirits
the Concord grapes
the work
of human hands
celebrating saints
worshiping one
in a mock royal robe
the burdens
the suffering
of this earth

that redeems
bar flies
pancake house patrons
firemen
builders
devout sisters
holy priests
late-shift nurses
at a restaurant
serving breakfast
24 hours a day
to the tired
and weak
the crosses
the passions
of ordinary people
are realized
and sometimes relieved

White Light

Light moves away
from crystals
colors disappear
from the walls.
the sun moves on
shooting beams
behind clouds

the brightest white
the radiance
a gleaming spectacle
a transfiguration
touching
the water forming
a lighted path
as if for a hiker
a rambler
a wanderer
with a walking stick
on flickering waves
like jumping molten silver
it points the way
a widening swath
to the stories
to hesitant tales
evading only
in moments
what constitutes
glorious light
the hues
reunited
recombined
in discovery
the revelations
of the visual
the mother word
in particulars
in wave lengths
specific objects
earth's lifeblood
where secrets
are no longer
kept all people
will know
in darkest corners
in the tightest cell
in miserable slums
the beginning
the middle
and the end
the theme
the verdict
uncovered sight
healed eyes
of justice
of mercy
the last pages
of age old mysteries
shining through

Uncertainty

Wind sends pollen
into the streets
like revolutionary peasants
it commands seagulls
to take an alternate route
over parking lots
They dance, sail
to new sideways
steps in the blue air.
The wind bends trees
so they look haunted
cruel, stooped
and crooked.
The ocean wind
is a force
to be reckoned
with relief
on a hot day
it is not human
but grinds the rocks
my untied hair
moves into knots; it slows
me down. I haven't
decided if it is friendly.

Segolene Royal

The woman wears white
a tailored jacket
for a French candidate
running for president
Who will tell her story
about what the sex
believes after having young?
She promises fairness, one
should be treated like
another.

That makes it difficult
to change directions
from old ways
the nurturing habits
reserved for children
A woman brings her whole
self wherever she goes.

She does not escape
history with success
It will not be easy
to find a world
that genuinely cares
with no favorites
but she would be there
in mighty decisions
in front of a microphone
standing on a platform
wrapped in state colors.

Bricks

Sandbur sunlight pricks
the turquoise clouds green,
and workers take bricks hard
and stack them into buildings
There is glory and white mud
on their shoes; they walk up the hill
and are celebrated for making
something that lasts beyond
bookmaker's conversations
and author notes. Their creation
will stand when the cloth hangs
in museums tourists people uncles
pass paying eight dollars to come in.

At 30 or 50

I thought I'd try
to tell stories
about fathers
and mothers
essences
on a daily drive
to where pelicans touch
the wild surf
so confident
and assured
I won't be
like a pelagic bird
that waits
for handfuls
of yellow popcorn
from weekend tourists
who leave
on Sunday.

What have I wanted?
the room with a writing table
the one across

from the river.
I am a child
of tar roads
of redwing blackbirds
once innocent
never taught
who looked
for interesting people
sharing ideas
lighting up
at the sound
of a beloved's name
or the person
who brought
birthday cakes
at 30 or 50
it was all
the same. It was all
the same, charming.
they used
that word
at a candidate's forum,

the perfect moderator
whom I loved.

I loved him, too.
the way
we see ourselves
without checked
paper boxes
fluid identity
where kings
and queens
are on the same table.

It is important
to talk of love now.
There seems
so little extra
a small serving
for everyone
people left hungry

in many ways
tired of neighbors
after years
of watching them
come and go
four hours away
where the green
stays forever
on the coast
with briny red roses
the winter is windy
and the buzzards
are chased off
with a broomstick
they do not impress me
the pelican takes what
is vital from the sea
never getting wet
until its dive
from the middle of the sky.

Chance Meeting

Now you are gone,
and I will never see
you again. How
was it that we came
to share the same
city and time
went to common
department stores
corner gas stations
sat at red lights
to view landmark buildings
while the traffic
passed people
keeping appointments
just to return home.
I can locate you
if I am silent hear
you laughing, drumming
up followers
in old neighborhoods
many hours
near Westminster
through lighted windows
the chase after holiness.

The Veil

I have a sheer veil
forgotten from one
who didn't get cold feet
but made a promise
and went to Tennessee
to the hilly land
near horse farms
high rises, music city
the item is long,
and it is not good
at covering imperfections.
I am not modest
I am not shy
I am rather outspoken
lift the material
almost see-through
the floor's sweep.

Vagabonds

Elderly people leave
too soon. They pack
up their bags
for auctions, sales
stocking hats
for bargain seekers
odorous sweaters
of an entire life
the remote control
in one spot
near the television,
and I miss them
their humble stories
told over again
with the same delight
in long distant calls
when everything
is explained
every family action
is reflected upon
and never missed.

Old people
take flight
and you might think
they are rude
to pick up their things
to go on a jaunt
they swoop through
the air glide
through eternity
play strategic cards
with roommates
They are hard to love
because they are fickle
canceling rain
drenched newspapers
neighbors bring
in the mail. You
never know when
they might skip town
carrying
their stories with them.

My Mother's Voice

I sing with my mother's voice
rich
deep
penetration
that goes beyond
our space
our time
into the past.
It cries
for our lovers
while nurturing
our children
concocting
sweet rhymes
that run
gush
pour
from our enclosures
our wombs
into stillness
into birth
into song

Winners and Losers

A bread heel
was left
after someone
fed the birds
six seagulls
discovered
the slice
on the pavement
of a favorite
tourist overlook
fluttering chaos
came next
each gull took
a turn holding
the prize
in its beak
until another
would fly in
and steal it
from its temporary owner
the exchange
went on for
a few minutes
until finally
a victor
flew away
with the piece
seemingly safe
over the water
but the cumbersome square
was too heavy
and dropped
into the sea.
only the lucky fish
didn't go without

Reminders

You will need
to provide us
with an email address
so we can send you
thoughtful reminders
our coupons
latest rewards
from sales meetings
from the people
who wear
company shirts
and call midday
about laminations
a completed order
team energy
a restless wind
the dogwood
petals fall
on the sidewalk
up to the steps
to the front
door nature
does not keep them
in the spam folder.

The Willow

I believe
in wind dances
and leaves
the way the sun
shines into
your eyes
and all is silver
and stretching out.

Then I remember
how hard
it is to love what
is explained
in books or not
explained in books.
How difficult
it is to stand
there letting trees
pass as drawings
pencil or ink
illustrations
rather than live

furrowed trunks.

I'm not complaining
but my thin rings
are numbered
in years and too many
times I've bent
to the ground
waiting for
the weather
to stop
so I could rise
and shake myself
straight
back stunned
and aching
and wondering why
the willow
sways sweeps
never falling
onto waiting grass.

Treacherous Road

The morning brings
a rare snowfall
the streets
salted for Southern
drivers who fire
up their engines
with imaginings
of a green flag
slick programs
with driver biographies
full beer coolers
the anticipation
deafening noise
the loud rumble
of the big race
and in some houses
the weatherman says
stores are closed
schools are empty
on account of ice
on sidewalks.
I will stay home
like the rest
and write opinions
for newspapers
in a furniture town
with two main drags
past churches
corporate headquarters
they have all
heard by now
that it is not safe.

Early Tree

A color wheel turns
in front
of a spotlight
onto silver
branches tinting
and reflecting a hue
in a crooked
little house
near an abandoned
rail station
never to become
a restaurant
it is a good thing
to remember

spirit pieces
and old friends
when the cedar seed
is broken
open memories
are pinched
living green
under curious nails
in a Midwestern town
where I visit
where I imagine
elderly furnace heat
and feel Christmas peace.

The Song of the Grackle

I

I hear a distant voice
that sounds like crickets
rubbing
their legs together
or ocean waves
throwing foam
at high tide.
It speaks to me.
It says move
from windy
and wet September
when roofs fly
from houses
and the president
is doing a public relations act.
The call once told me
to follow
a bright star
and hide out
in barns
at evening meet friendly
  neighbors
who shared the values
of freedom.

It speaks
to me about liberty
cut chains put
on by a master
many masters
or whoever owns
the land
the jet planes tanks
that can't be
in the big parade
because they tear
up streets.
The voice cries
it commands
it says march
to even ballerinas
in contemporary
  choreography
downtown Los Angeles
or cultural hubs
in the middle of pancake
  flatlands
it tells me
to put tennis shoes

on swoosh three stripes
lace tightly
then step on hardwood floors
where the sea
is only blocks away
the river
is a two-day drive
past cornfields
the dirt is black
productive
making farmers rich
on paper. The noise sounds
like a tractor running
turning soil
in measured rows
after people came
from Sweden
with two pairs
of pants, a coat
to go into the coal mines
or to plow
the owners'
land with horses
the pictures
in black and white
of men
with cough drop
brothers' beards
the clear instruction
is to leave all
that is comfortable
scenic for the sake
of release
from would-be despots
who scapegoat
the weak
and disconnected
the country quilt-maker
who takes fabric squares
into a warm design
a mix of colors
a mix of people
no longer free.

The woman sits
in an office
the sounds of traffic
from a city
where the poor stand out
on street corners
knocking on car windows
asking for change.

The coffers
are empty drivers
are broke
paying bills online
until they
are penniless
The sound of tires
of speed
the race
of rush hour
sounding
against barrier walls
say move leave
travel down
the highway
to a grassy meadow
far from the rats
that tease
outdoor felines
from a place where
the taxes are high
and the water
is poison
with lead
aging infrastructure
the roads

crumble
except
the tar one
smooth bubbling
impressionable
oily iridescent soles
the black can only
be removed
with lighter fluid
that is past
and everybody knows
it. No more Pall Mall
diseased lungs
for carpet-layers
and Singer sewing machine
salesmen
now long gone
the voice came in like
pine needles sweeping
the wind.
It is time
to get out
or before I know it
no one
will believe in
anything

higher
than a party's platform
with balloons
confetti distractions.
Can I walk away?
Can you depart?
The words say clearly
that the shoes
are worn
but must go
they've been places
to horse fields
in Kentucky
to Rocky Mountains
where hummingbirds
drink grenadine
to a land joined
by rivers
and separated
by governmental borders
to coastal communities
where dogs
are not allowed
on the beach strand.

The desire to move
hasn't left me.
I hear the bells
from the university peal
they say get on
from landmark buildings
to a view
of Old Main
of the Mississippi
of the water, always
flowing
around
a fallen tree
making its way
with the current
pools swirling
around jutting
branches.
I always come home
I have roots
like a poplar
knobby wooden arms
extending down
the shiny mud banks meeting
the wide stream.

I dream of pilgrims
the voyagers
who wanted religious
   freedom
independence
the right to believe
walk for rights
to be unbound
to imagine democracy
in place
move step high
journey
into the night
looking at the sky
your star cosmic
and full
of destiny. Join
the voices
the beginning
of choirs
with sopranos
alto
tenor
and bass
booming
at traffic stops
being heard
at noisy rabbles
for festive audiences
in the quiet homes
where the elderly couple live
on Social Security
in churches
when the congregation
has gone
went about
daily routines
I dream this,
that democracy
will hold
in a nation
that thinks
on its own
and the truth
is sacred.

Move for the love
of children
restless
fidgety
crying
unsuspecting heirs

when scientists issue
their reports
about man-made
climate change
they were taught
to deny
to ignore
to fabricate
and are expected now
to solve problems.
They will
want to step
away from
wildfires
droughts
floods
they will be
a displaced people
who will want
to go home
wanting rootedness.

The country
is not your own.
Be on your way.
Yesterday's flag
was to fight
and die
for don't tread
on me
or make
me believe
in causes, causes
are lost. Put on
tawny leather boots
to the calves
to walk miles in
go quickly
through dense forests
across chilly deserts
through meadow lanes
to town hall
city streets
like forbearers
who believed
in the right
of people to live
in harmony
after a contest
the better wins
in faraway wars
suspended rifles

and bayonets
peace comes
from battles legs
are amputated
from running at
a fortified fence
the rubber tires burn
are purposely
set on fire
smoke
blackening
obscuring
the air
the sight
the target
the enlisted
one hears
the cries say
move on, take
what is left
of principle
and call
your mother
she will
not answer
the years

have passed
she is no longer young
and victorious
the government paycheck
still covers bills
for the kid's
dental work
for fuel oil
long after
the conviction
the reason
the people
left mourning.

New Zealand's
celebrated citizen
breaks away
from the father
the local patriarch
in Wellington
society get-togethers
satin dresses
a changed name
Katherine Mansfield
the rebel
who travels

to London
and will marry
a critic. The past
is scandalous
the future
more promising
no regrets
praise
to a maternal
grandmother
childhoods spent
at the beach
with little voices
the visual made alive
with words
the feeling of bliss
the moon shining
on the pear tree
the claimed sexuality
then a beloved
brother killed
in the service
the girl known
in her own right
for stories
She 'd move

to the country
for cures
tending cows
spotted wings
with tuberculosis
with a guru
a health advisor
the march complete
at a very young age

The life stayed
in my mind
a literary outsider
with Woolf
the crazy woman
the only one now
certain to be
in the canon
a female wonder
someone
to dream of being like
the humor
the seriousness
the gossip
of Bloomsbury
retold in diaries

March for sanity
for a woman's genius
one half woman
the other half
necessary
to create
wholeness
incandescence
a Times review
a curious trip
to Haworth
to see
Bronte's small shoes

traveling
to Brussels
walk to our mothers
march to them
with a glued spine
in paperback
in an electronic format
the old man
outlives
his children
and shoots the sky
in a churchyard at night.

II

Go when you can.
Pray they don't find gold
on ancestral lands
profiteers
government officials
will move tribes
the strong
the now hearty
the elderly
the sick
will be relocated.
Others can dig deep
into the earth
and pull
out cash
for ornate buggies
ten room houses
the familiarity
the culture
is lost
displaced
as a whole people
walk cross
state lines
to a reserve special
the chief
is replaced
with a governor
a warrior marries
a woman
of German stock.
It must be said.
I say it.
Take another way
for past injustice
the dust
of the moccasin
it rises
it chokes
it dirties
around steps
from Georgia
to Oklahoma. Do
not forget
what good men
will do for money
the tears do
not belong

to community leaders
talking compassion
give reasons spin
the truth.
Greedy people
officials
explaining cruelty
to a weary public
who always want
to believe
in best intentions,
who want
not to be
bothered
or become involved.

The potato crop fails
the Great Hunger
a million people starve
a million leave
their homes.
The plants' leaves turn black
like corpses
from a blight
but the citizens
foolishly
export food
nourishment
sweet butter
to the landowners
who sit
in legislatures
and pass laws
to benefit the few.

The body
grows weak
is susceptible to illness
What offence
do the poor commit
to watch loved ones die
wither away
waste? Where
is the mercy
of God
when one
is forced
to march, to leave
the graves
of ancestors
and the newly dead?

Go on, lift the legs
find a better circumstance
Do not wait
to be forced
when nobody hears
the ballot is pale
shadowy cold
like Northern sunlight
the election
is rigged
votes uncounted
and the heart
bursts with sentiment
against oppressors
wearing wingtips
pin-striped suits
the hegemony
of privilege
of connection
of networks
of silk
of gold
of fossil fuels pumping
in the neighbor's yard.
Speak now

the mechanical see-saw
or the tunnels
for coal burnt
in the open air
tower-like clouds
toxic thunderheads
red hot bituminous rocks
   cooled
in a lake
tainted fish
selenium, mercury
where people
play water sports
and drink beer.

I can talk of nicer things
but my eye
is on the light
my ear
on the voice
It reminds me
of a kinder place
where supper
is served to all people
the laughter

of ordinary folks
who work
in the factories
for 20 years

and name their children
after handsome
and popular
TV celebrities.

III

I walk
by roses
and wonder why
they open
as full as frosted rolls
when planted
in the garden.
Everything beautiful
calls out
to stand up
to witness
to not let ugliness
go unmentioned.
A star ray guides me.
It makes me think
of the others
when the world
was unbearable
causing sufferers
to carry through,
to keep walking
to carry the cross
My knowledge
of footpaths
of trails
of gravel roads
will help find
where freedom
abounds.

I hear the chimes
of clocktowers
and the hands
are moving
like my legs across
stony ways.

I search through
memories
my stories
that instruct
biographies
of heroines
and saints
the earth's womb
speaks to me.

I have heard
of the wise
doctors of philosophy
professors
theologians
St. Teresa Benedicta of the
 Cross
who died
at the orders
of sinful men.
Do you see
this era
with its pervasive lies
and self-serving notables?
The sound says march.

I heard of a woman
who led an army
a young leader
professing her Grace
she was called
a heretic
a witch
for her military prowess.
I heard of a man
who believed in Truth
who led
a rebel movement
spontaneous
participants
for hours
for days
people
would walk
to make salt
from the ocean
to gain national
independence
nonviolent
resistance
the actions
that brought low
British rulers
who hoarded power.
The sea is listening
and talking.

This is the song
of the grackle.
Its chatter and clicks
are annoying
to the songbird

and painted bunting
It is not for the extraordinary
the celebrated
the coveted. It
is a song
that sounds pretty
to a common beach
bird brown
and shiny black
with an open beak
and yellow eyes.
Its song
is for everyone
discounted
poor and hard
to love.
The noisy fuss
in the middle
of grassy dunes
and sea oats
must say march
in a resonating pitch
for waitresses
the postman
the elevator mechanic
the window cleaner
the custodian
the sanitation worker
to whoever else
is unheard.
It's a song
that cannot
be denied or forgotten
It is a lovely song
to its kind.
The grackle loves
the grackle's tune.

It says move, march
over the bridge
at Selma
with troopers
present. Never
forget the 30-something man
with a gift
for oratory
for wisdom
and courage
who inspired people
to walk
to forbidden places
to demand

a say
a ballot
when there
was anger
in the dominant heart.
Forgive
the brutality
of clubs
of shouts
of curses
when people
don't love
as they should
imagining
the robbery
of good things
too much scarcity
the other
is the night's thief.

I have heard
of a time
when women
couldn't practice law
when they
did research
in the backroom.
Their voices
never rose
in courtrooms.

My great-grandmother
couldn't vote
when she turned 21.
She took photographs
of her brothers
in doughboy uniforms
they were off
to a war
in which
she had no say. I turn
the album's pages
and I say step
for every
girl child
who realized
few dreams.

My father broke lamps
to get my mother's attention
to announce
his displeasure

They were expensive
gold-toned
with crystal
But he didn't think
she heard him.

The politicians shock
with their words.
Some thought
equality
was written
in stone
like settled law. Take
to the open
young women
without
generations
of wealth
or financial
backers.
Or those people
who were packed
into ships
to middle passage
the advantage
is slippery

uncertain
a gambler's bet
an era can take
it away.

Abigail Adams
knew about
the desire
for power.
It never relents.
It is never
satisfied
and it is not given
up without
struggle people
do not rest
swing the legs
to the side
of the bed
awaken
my friend
from slumber
put them
on the hard ground
open the door
and walk in crowds.

Thousands
of black birds
take off
to pepper
the late summer sky,
airy ribbons twisting
turning
the migration
a spectacle
the move
to ample food
Let us go
like a flock
or a thunderous herd
staying together.
Who knows
what can happen?
I am reminded
of a sea
that opened
to a people.
I am reminded
of the women
who badgered
their husbands
at dinnertime
disobeying
the rules
of proper ladies.

The fertile minds
at universities
argue theories
aren't restrained.
I believe
in the force
of notions
of books
of science
of conclusion
something higher
than rhetoric
only meant
to persuade.

Advertising worlds
will relent
the agenda
won't be
about profit
silk-pocketed men
will go home

The Song of the Grackle • 223

to spend time
with families.

The light appeals to me
The voice whispers
in my ear
to move
keep going
the many
in unison
like a hundred slaves
who made a pact

not to be put down
in chains
in shackles
but to seek a place
where all could be heard
in the daylight
with a hundred light
points cast
on the walls
the brilliant sunshine.
revealed.

IV

This is the house of light
with windows
in every direction
it enfolds me
uncovers me
emboldens
with its spirit gained
from churches
from a gift rosary.
I have said
my prayers
the commandment
is to step
people come out
from what binds
walk in pairs
or the footprints
of thousands
marking the road
a footpath
when the clouds rain
when they
do not rain
and dust rises
around soles
the movement
of grackles
through the sky
of revolutionaries
of rebels
of the ordinary
who want what
is better
more truth
more facts
a free press
more democracy
more justice
in a failing world.

I can talk
of happier times
a child is born
emerges
the pain stops
with naming. Give
the sentiment
a word

a meaning
an introduction
something
to be called
from infancy
recognition
the baptismal water
of beginnings
of schooling
of higher degrees
worked on
for a decade.
Who will say?
Who will listen?
Who will care?
The right words
will be spoken
are waited
for like an Atlantic
waterwheel
pushing itself
with energy
natural force
expelling
seven lucky
dolphins
that swim
in the rushing
the retreating spray
near granite rock.

My ear hears
words following words.

I have heard
of a woman
who lived among
the poor
asking for nothing
but the approval
of God
nursing
the lesions
of unloved humanity.
They called
her holy
because caring
is an extraordinary effort
that is empathy
that is compassion
when others
can't see it.

The crowd does
not roar
or applaud
a lack
of self interest
the buying season
is extended
from October
to December time
to spend
to buy gifts
to part
with cash
for the hiring
of part-time
workers
who are without benefits
or a vacation
to a tropical island
or a motel deep
in the mountains
of Tennessee.

The hero's
heart pumps fast
it anticipates

the danger
of drought
of high temperatures
to structures.
The inferno
is stoked
by Santa Ana winds
it descends
it engulfs
leaving no trace
of blueprints' design
of best dreams.

People flee
they march
to a safer existence.
A warning goes
out. Take notice
that the earth
has limits
is restricted
in the amount
of abuse
it can take.
The sirens' sound
repeatedly

then are over.
A planet means business,
and people
will act differently
or die.

I have heard
of a man
who wanted
to be alone
and lived
by a pond, chronicling
the natural world
The man didn't pay
his taxes,
couldn't support
an unjust war.
He went
to jail maybe
a star ray led him
or he heard
the call
that is in my mind.
It takes
into account
that daffodils
bloom
in clusters
after being alone.

The idea will grow
it will prompt
the grackle
to fly where
the summer
and winter
are sustainable, looking
to be vital
for the next year.
A chocolate
chip sky stirred
in the white air,
mass movement
the sight
of a higher will.

This is the song
of the grackle,
or the house
of light
the scent
of clover

in a Midwestern field
the light purple
flowers
that are sweet
to the taste.
They call the bees
and grazing animals
that depend
on open land.
Walk outside
from low
or tall
buildings
down
stairs one step
after another
keep a pace
but find patience
deliberation
resolve.
Find the reason
to move
to travel
a days' drive
in the sound
of the wind

lightly blowing
small columbines
or the Indian paintbrush
on a hikers' trail.

I hear the voice
in the rustling aspens
in a rush
of mountain air
wind chimes tinkle
and the broken rock popping
under tires
on the road
on the shoulder
of winding turns
the message '
comes up
silently now
through the chest
a repetition
a strong suggestion.
I listen intently
to coursing utterances
quietly spoken
in the body
in cutting sensation

to the center
to the mind.
It is emphatic
will not be ignored.
I ask to hear again
the talk between chatty
  angels
and falling stars
the noise
they must make
to enter
the atmosphere
still quite fiery
making onlookers wonder
if the sound
if the sight
can be counted on.

V

If a tree falls in the forest
does it say march
move for brothers
and the sisters
who taught
at Catholic colleges
for 30 years
and decided
they loved women?
When one
is alone
outside
of tradition
of institutions
of creeds
and everything
that upholds patriarchy
the sound
the light
the migration
will seem reasonable.

Go now others
will follow
shake off expectations
assumptions
or facts
that deal in the flesh.
Leave the past
its nightmares
the fathers
who never buy
dog food products
for a bloated mongrel
that is hidden
that is loved
that is dying
in the attic
in walk-ins
the caves
kept in houses.

Unhand me
memories
moving pictures

it releases me
from the bondage
of oppressors
who want
their way
in the home
with thermostats
with light switches
in the church
in politics. I say
again, I will be free
and will loosen
the fetters
of others.

VI

A new tender plant
will grow
from77 a field
of ashes.
The earth
will cool
from its fever
on the day
everyone hears
the fluttering
of feathers
of bird wings
the prophecy
of the grackle
that is not
so pretty
to witnesses
without shiny tailfeathers.

I have heard
of an art critic
who retold the story
of the vineyard
the workers

who went in late
and were paid
the same.
"The only wealth
is life," the life
of power-brokers
who give
to campaigns
to universities
and those beggars
who stand
in intersections
holding signs. They say,
I am hungry
I am without
the famine
is with us
until the buds
are fresh, new
and reappear
on the smoldering trees.

History might save
the world

The Song of the Grackle • 233

protect it
from those given power
who ignore
disregard
the well-being
of thousands.
Certainly, they fall
like statues
the memorialized
who are no
longer chic
pulled forward
to the hard ground.

The collective brain
that keeps liberty
is tucked away
in the vault
firing synapses
when necessary
about how far
we've come
from forgiving
atrocities
the canisters
that go off
on the border
the children crying
or squirming
in the sanctuary
standing
on shoulders
to see consecrated bread.

I will depend on the mythos
the pattern
of people's minds
the psychology
of masses
of folks
to discern
that which favors
freedom.
The song
of the grackle
becomes loud,
present
calling listeners
to move
to step
to dance
to walk

to its common tune.
The fields
will turn green
with crops
that feed
the hungry.
The land
will bear fruit
trees heavy
with plums
or apples.
The star's fire
will give light
showing off
the dark night's path.
The bird
will take flight
over the seeded earth.

Come to the bountiful table
that stretches
across every
comet-streaked sky
with roasted meats
with warm breads
no more scapegoats
or guilty people
pass the baskets
of plenty. See
the morning river.

March, you
are welcomed home.

The Magnificent Light of Morning

Preface

On January 6, 2021, democracy was violently assaulted. Rioters, fed lies, invaded the Capital Building where Congress convened to certify the presidential election results. Led by a sitting president, it was an unsuccessful coup. Its infamy is lasting and its perpetrators are not gone.

As an American citizen, the siege was heartbreaking. As a poet, the event called me to a greater appreciation of my craft, because language leans toward the truth. The act of creating a poem requires exactness when choosing words. The poetic process cannot err as the bard assumes the role, the responsibility of witnessing events, ideas, and even objects in society. The mind's eye sees a small thing with four wheels. In the poet's quest for accurate naming, he or she decides if it is a wagon or a cart; it is a wagon, thus the repeated decision-making about word choice results in truth. In times of turmoil, the poet's work becomes necessary and essential.

The 20th Century poet Carl Sandburg said that poetry is "a synthesis of hyacinths and biscuits." His description is seemingly discordant; it does not seem to make sense. Sometimes people say that they don't understand poetry. Poetry is such a close form, meaning the only thing between the wordsmith and paper might be God. It focuses on the human interior, the poet's being. It's proximity to the poet's inner self, not only makes sense, it's impossible to lie.

For that reason, the authoritarian regime often targets poetry because it defies propaganda.

The Magnificent Light of Morning is a synthesis of the public and the private realm, the secular and the sacred. Prompted by Lacanian psychoanalytic theory, it explores time as history, being male, or the Symbolic, and fluidity as female, or the Semiotic. In it, I confront domestic and institutional violence, contrasting these aspects with the calming characteristics of nature.

I thank my husband John, a healer, Dennis Sampson, a poet, and the literary women who have all helped me become a better artist. I'm grateful for my constant God; I believe truth is sacred.

Mattie McClane, February 2, 2021, Wilmington, NC

"In the shortest sea voyage there is no sense of time. You have been down in the cabin for hours, days, or years. Nobody knows or cares... You do not believe in dry land any more-you are caught in the pendulum itself, and left there, idly swinging."

– Katherine Mansfield

"Water does not resist. Water flows. When you plunge your hand into it, all you feel is a caress. Water is not a solid wall, it will not stop you. But water goes where it wants to go, and nothing in the end can stand against it … Remember that you are half water. If you can't go through an obstacle, go around it. Water does."

— *Margaret Atwood*

"She looked into the distance, and the old terror flamed up again for an instant, then sank again. Edna heard her father's voice and her sister Margaret's. She heard the barking of the old dog that was chained to the sycamore tree. The spurs of the cavalry officer clanged as he walked across the porch. There was the hum of bees, and the musky odor of pinks filled the air."

— Kate Chopin, The Awakening

"War is a man's game … the killing machine has a gender, and it is male."
— Virginia Woolf, *Three Guineas*

The Magnificent Light of Morning

I

I leave the lake triumphant
old signs present
and cooled
by the clear water July days,
nights
the time
is suspended hour-like
minutes
every noticed clock
an amazement
How could it be?
We have laughed played until
the air turns gray
from lack
of sunlight night creeps
becomes alive
on the wild shores
animals make
their move undetected
by the resting boaters
perfectly tanned
in preparation
for the work day
office politics
the snub falls away
does not last
because youth
is brilliant
assured
of opportunity offers
before the wing
is constructed across
from an art gallery
with this day there
is hope resilience
what the body and mind
gather
from myths
from Ponce de Leon
the fountain searched for
for a lifetime
the white cream removes
lines
and long repeated stories
the listener pauses
there is politeness
or indifference

It's hard to tell which
what is true.

I remember a cheap
window covered
with frost cold wet
to the touch on
the inside
where the furnace coughed
the rest
is told in pictures
attempts
to capture
stop time
from ruining afternoons
yellowing
albums bought
in easy installments
to see where
desire began small
simple thoughts
grow become graduate papers
but keep going
like worn shoes
detached
from the leather
its strings
the legs
are strong
have walked
around paths
since beginnings
of distilleries
and billboards.

Time brings the morning.
Where do we go from here?

The golden light escapes
the cloudbank
is calling moments forward
in a white dress
First Communion
another picture
bucking time
stopping
to record
and satisfy grandparents
the grandfather's
one suit reserved
for occasions
where food and drink

are served
to a group
to relatives
to friends
to neighbors
at the capacity appropriate
venue
a shell-shocked preacher
is there with cakes
past the expiration
dates free
and loaded
into a Volvo trunk
at the local grocery store.
Time allows him
to tell stories years later
when the mind
shrinks holding
the important
three elements
of the trauma
over and over again
What does
time care anyway?
No, time doesn't tear up
for lost puppies

or any memories
of men with blown faces
from a war
that everyone came
to and left less whole.
No one should
call time father
It is thirty-something
and a born leader
It leads politicians
to rail against
term limits.
they were
just elected
time passes
and they haul out
the old signs, asking
for votes. Time
is a marker. Love
does not matter
to it. It has no intention
of returning
affection.
Every real lover
knows timing
is always bad

but time changes minutes
in a beloved's presence
the clock
then speeds
to the parting slows
to eternity
when waiting
for reunion.
But don't think it cares
or wants to make life easy
for foolish hearts.

Snow hangs
from the gutters
like rolls
of white paper
on downtown stores
cover sidewalks
the roofs
of cars hidden
and elevated
from whiteness.
The boy is ten
on his way home
from buying dry beans
and coffee. He rests
in the snow,
keeping
his mother's receipt
in a gloved hand.
He becomes aware
of his life
of a heart beating
cheeks stinging
from a windy freeze.
time pauses
It will let him wonder
about his existence.

Time knows the poor
always waiting
anxiously dreaming
for something better.
Time holds a check
on the first
of the month
the mother
giving a watchful eye
when a milk jug
is half empty
with every swallow
because there might

not be money
for schools supplies
picking them out
in make believe
because charity
makes pencils free
binding thoughts
mending ways
of kind persons
or cold government
offers. Time
dampens fantasy hope
when the goods
are all the same
year after year
the child grows
becomes a man
writing on the back
of cereal boxes
the perfect poem.

A 1960s model car
is parked outside

of an educational
testing center
where the night passed
with thoughts
of briefs decisions
the wish for a shower
the fatigue
the brain-drain
after hours of filling
in the blank
sometimes doubt
sometimes ease
the answer
comes quickly
with everything at stake
the test booklet goes
into a wastebasket
then crank the starter
the long drive across
the windy prairie
its long grass
to a large frame duplex
housing three children

II

Military dreams
every man a hero packed
into amphibious
war machines
above bombers practice
the sky's roar
of engines
in formation
for the next conflict
where soldiers freeze
in the winter
the wished for
discipline
of loners
who confide
in the family dog
and live
with three
headstrong women.

The household
is grieving
is a place
to be avoided
on a wintry trek.
The flag covers
the casket talk overheard
that the family
is bent over
in grief
others
passing by
like horror
like plague
like fever
is in the home
near the train station.

Time knows the rich suits
with cut flowers
on the lapel.
A soloist's voice fills
the theater
front row seats
in a pre-pandemic scene
walls are erected
with words
and not knowing

other possibilities.
The minutes begin ticking
to another place
another season
another harvest
with the silos filled
with grain
that make
fine bourbon
to pass the common
unextraordinary hours
with a portrait
on yard signs
time finally a success.

Let's hear it for patriarchy
Or not.
for bold institutions
military might
ranked men
systematic hierarchies
our fathers
also had fathers
to model
and imitate people
who do not cry

often except in country songs
where they
are considered outlaws.
the car keys thrown
into a field
on a grassy bluff
for punishment
from a drunken man
blame goes out
but cruelty
is not experienced
only the topic
of stories
about boyhood
I have spoken against you
I've been critical
I have let the world
know my story
and have
seldom considered
yours. Time makes
us reflective
when there
is no other recourse
I surrender hurt
to whoever reads books

or imagines children
left behind.

Time knows the middle-class
two income families crowd
into swimming pools
the trees line
subdivisions
two cars
in the driveway
of a two-story house
with a TV
in the living room
watching sports
rooting
for teams
the call
is to stay home
with an elderly dog
and buy groceries
from Walmart ordered
from a phone
that takes portrait
photographs
of children playing
at the beach.

The gray thunder booms
and rolls above
the Sargasso Sea
that changes
with every sight
with wind direction
with shifting sands
sometimes smooth
sometimes blue
the water jumps
and bounces
as brown water
as Coke bottle green
is never the same
it never bores
the imagination
I meditate
on its many appearances
eternal body
lasting flow charging
the shore. I feel closer
to a Midwestern home
to a constant God
and a myrtle grove.

The gulls are watchful
Their turning gaze
seems short
mechanical
as they perch
on seven posts
birds eyeing parked cars
their drivers
their passengers
What can they report
in their chatty
language?
Are there love scenes
to ponder
to gossip about
surfers carrying
their boards
with the profound conviction
that nobody drowns?

Fence pickets on the ground
the hurricane
does not spare
the boats
in the marina
cut loose tossing
in the spray trees down
at both ends
of the block.
The sound
of chainsaws greet
the morning
there is triumph
in the air
the sky is blue now
Time passes
into a new day.

III

I wait for the yellow boat
I walk to the point craning
my neck
to the East
a girl looking
for the beloved
the smell
of tobacco
of oil-mixed fuel
in a small V-bottom
cutting through
summer waves rescuing
from boredom
onlookers
who think
my attention
is too young.
I only know
the sharp bends
of the Green River
the thrill
of a motor defying
the current
around

partially sunken logs
causing the water
to swirl
in jagged
liquid lines
while cows graze
on the high ledge banks.
This is the time I want
a channel
so narrow
so full
so fast
that the flow rushes
past exposed
tree roots
into the wider stream.

The deep scar
on the shoulder
a purple heart
for a marine
for a boy
who was on the swim team
in a mill town

and learned
a carpenter's trade
rebuilding flood
damaged homes
not yet put on stilts.
A brother comes home
in a body bag
someone receives
a perfectly
folded flag
put on bookshelves
while the old man
waits for time
to heal misfortune
the survivor
the man
in the yellow boat
is without stories
is without
children moving
to dairy country.

Time is indifferent
not crying until
it meets academia
the historian

the biographer
giving a narrative
to letters
in storage boxes
in libraries
special collections
the work
of lifetimes
with a call number
He would not phone.
He would not answer.
The loves that are
in dreams
and absent spilt
the river
at the bow. Where
do we go
from here
with the water cut in two?
The wake spreads
to the shore
each side
each wave going
its own way
rocking tied vessels
and little water-logged twigs

The Magnificent Light of Morning • 257

that rise
that float
that hop
onto ground. They are
freed from the endless
bobbing
a monotonous motion
the unrest
in people's hearts
the political divides
that separate
when everyone proclaims
patriotism while
the hatred surges.

It is better to wait for
the yellow boat
even while drunkards sit
on barstools
everyone
is called a nickname
Whiskey Bob
or Indian Charlie
who profess
to the audience
that friends

are like butter
in the sun
unreliable sots
telling stories
by campfires
near the marina
bull frog lore
the night's chorus
until each fall asleep
under a clear sky.

A flock of pelicans
fly over the house
They are back
from plunging
into January's sea.
All creatures
are hungry
near the ocean
the tides
are predictable
I put on readers
to know
the news finding
once again people
who are needy. Yes, I told

you time knows
with the poor
When is the rent due?
The money does
not go far enough
the hunger
is in children
in dignity
the recognition
that one cannot wait
for lawmakers
to learn compassion
when the world
is political busy
offering lip service
to appear morally engaged.

Test scores come back
the man runs for Justice
of the Peace.
He drives too fast
is ticketed
rebuked
in a local newspaper
and then
tells his wife
that he's leaving her
for better things.
I just wait
for the yellow boat.
It comes to me
on quiet nights
when the stars shine
when the neighbor's
television
is on and can be
seen through
the blinds
I have always
liked getaway
crafts or whatever else
shows the way out
down wild fast rivers
a sharp turn
to the outdoors.
I once lived in a place
without water
three-day schedules
rationing
to hose down
the thirsty grass.
Like clockwork,

the clouds let down
scatter drops
on tennis courts
in the afternoon
the Chinook winds
quickly dry them
while legislators argue
about rights
to the Colorado river.

The long journey
is over mountains
to find
a frigid lake
near backroad shacks
where hermits
make plans
play out sieges
in their minds
and read anti-government
leaflets
an only subscription.
Why is the world so mad?
It does not anticipate
any vessel
to free itself
from grievance
the complaints add up
the lost father
the man on the cross
the doubt-filled Thomas
in a junk strewn
rocky village
on the way to ski resorts.

Time knows the rich
money is speech
drowning
campaign coffers
until every candidate
is sponsored
by a personal
billionaire
who gives up
on multi-million
dollar homes
thousand-acre ranches
extended family
compounds
for power
for influence
for control

money changes
the world, buries
the utterances
of ordinary men
too much
inequality
graciously
acknowledged
accepted
by stockholders

insider trading
for the souls
the hides
the muscles
the respect
of the less fortunate.

Time deals with them
with the threat of the mob.

IV

The shell-shocked preacher
counsels
veterans
post traumatic
stress patients
who have lost limbs
experiencing
phantom pain
the soldiers
who do not sleep
at night for fear
of the sights
the sounds
of battle. Nightmares
are too frequent
the wives are gone
seeking better
calmer nerves
Time knows
the suffering. No day
old bread
can cure what ails
the haunted
the war torn.

Free doughnuts
are all he can bring
while men go
over the hill
looking for the magnificent
light of morning.

Let's hear it for patriarchy
Or not.

He opens a practice
in a country town
then drinks
too much
sits on town councils
noon lunches
with bankers
while he clenches
the woman's breast
in his fist pulling
and twisting it
spitting curses
He leans over
her kicking

his heavy shoes
at her ankle
until it breaks. The
police come and go.
The officers do
not interfere.

I walk to the point looking
for the yellow boat
that cruises down
the river
past cabins
fish tails swirl
making circles
prompting eddies
on a wet fabric
in the stretch
of stream
where poplars'
green leaves
reflect on
the surface
of water going, moving
to the roller dam.

I cannot see it. I cannot see it.
Tomorrow, I'll return.

I will return
and wonder
if there is not enough
testosterone
in the world
for patriarchs
for military men
for would-be autocrats
for those who play
with balls
give concussions
crunch bones
bruise muscles
on a Saturday afternoon.
Time knows
the brute
Darwinian instincts
the toughest
the strongest
who train
who work
to oppress

to dominate
and prey
on weaker creatures.
Time knows
more than
one man
who would
be Lenin willingly
without pity.

V

Women might not count
on the Church.
Gregorian chants
in baritone
the sacred liturgy
the order
of bishops
the Most Holy Father
says she can only read verse
at Mass
is restricted
relegated to the chairs
near the back
of the cathedral
while priests file
in at an installation.
Everyone has a place
in the hierarchy
not of heaven
but of robed men
who are called
to an exclusive vocation
brothers all.
She is like
the unnamed woman
who met Jesus
on the way
to crucifixion
"Only weep
for yourself
and your children."

Time knows a constant God
who speaks in the calm of
water.

I look at a first love
I didn't think
of a scarred shoulder
the white marred skin.
It did not
signify war
or aggression.
It had nothing to do
with hate
no foreign
relation's
failures

only the joy
of a man
who loved the water.

Frost melts
in golden
sunlight
glimmering rays
of morning
release
the frozen
slough.
After due
consideration
second loves
are women
Woolf
Chopin
Naslund
who return
to water
to amniotic
fluids
the wombs
of mothers
embrace

the incessant
rocking
the depth
solid
tight
wholeness
to warm
enclosure
seeking
the healer
above all things.

The healer steps
into the river
is immersed
in baptismal springs
the world hopes
offers prayers
in silence
for a gentler way
a man stands
at the podium
fireworks shoot
into the sky
the father
is pleased

the son renewed
as the people
anticipate
an alternative
to the broken past.

It's the victory of water.
It's the victory of light.

To Free the Sisters of Mary

Preface

I was listening to Adrienne Rich's recorded poetry reading from the 1990s, and she referenced the "women's liberation movement." In 2021, the words seem antiquated, as if women have moved past the need to be freed. The truth is women now occupy space in most professions.

They are doctors and lawyers. They are elected to legislative halls and vote on important bills, affecting global policies. Yet, young girls are affronted with celebrity icons who are popularly compelled to bare their bodies, supporting the idea that women are still majorly objectified in in culture. Patriarchy still informs women's identities, making them unfree, unequal, and thus unsafe.

There is a continued need to liberate women from the accepted cultural norms that promote violence and often hidden forms of oppression. Women will not be free or safe anywhere in the world until the Catholic Church with its 1.3 billion worldwide members changes its views and allows women to be ordained as deacons and priests. Women do not have equal status in the Church, therefore culture.

The Catholic Church participates wittingly or unwittingly in widespread misogyny. In the past, feminist women have left the Catholic Church rather than insist it change its ideas. In more cynical moments, I think the Church hierarchy welcomes their departure; the headache is gone. Yet the Catholic Church cannot exist without the help of millions of ordinary women. Everyday Catholic women can demand change; and the world changes, when we free sisters of Mary.

Mattie McClane, December, 2021, Wilmington, North Carolina

I

The power is out
in New Orleans
from Hurricane Ida
a mighty river reverses
its course. Will young
men prophesy
and the old dream
of signs? It is a time
to proclaim
that the world
will be new
with its powerful CEOs
in coats
and opened shirts
the relaxed look
there are no
more obstacles
to fairness. They
have consumed
enough taken
mashed sweet potato
from the toddler's mouth.
The light is coming
for you, from a mountain
with three tents
you shall see it
a dazzling spectacle
and share a secret
that will be known
in time, when all
is known
the busy bodies
who broadcast
the news
will be struck
mute from tireless
forecasting
self-serving pundits
in search of the big job
in prime time.
How much
do they pay
for you to spout
the agreed upon script
in a country
that has grown
accustomed
to falsehoods?
What is it
your children

put on school forms
when ask what
you do for a living?
Mine is a fabricator
a storyteller
for corporations
for a member
of Congress
great professions
that are bought
and sold. Turn off
the big box
that noise maker
of mass communication
of the people
who would
not rewrite history
but yesterday's happenings
or that
of weeks ago
or months ago
when the eyes
still remember
and are not healed.

I recall a documentary
about China
when its government
would put
loudspeakers
at the top
of street poles,
indoctrinating
spreading
the party's news.
In our country,
we turn them on
in living rooms. The
host's lead voice
interviews others
all speculation
all guessing
all narratives
to affect
to manipulate
power standings
a second
Catholic president
beaten down
by daily criticism.

Have we so
quickly forgotten
who came before him?
We have not forgotten
but someone's profit
is ailing,
is falling
the chaos sells
when people
only want
to go for a walk
to fall in love
hum melodies
have birthday parties,
the loss
of private lives
to public strife.

I have watched
democracy diminished.
I have seen millionaires
become billionaires
while people survive
on donated food.
I will say
that it is over,
the great inequality.
In my imagination,
I hear you laugh
a chuckle
then a roar.
Who am I, you say
to declare
such a change
in fortune?
I am a witness
I am a poet
I am a proclaimer
like when
Lincoln announced
the slaves were free
through
the Emancipation
Proclamation or when
Luther tacked
his thesis to
the Church's door.
It needs
to be stated,
it needs to be said
before it happens.
The long term

design
the plan
that isn't mine
is put in motion
no one
really denies
that some
should not go hungry
while others invite
friends on space flights.

Please understand
that the only tool
I have is words. They
won't numb
you like vodka
but you will
want a shot
after you see
the truth
in them.
You will huddle
with cohorts
and wonder what
is to be done. You
will hide them, erase

them, knowing
somewhere
in your mind
in the history of silence
"that truth
crushed to earth
will rise again."
A man said that,
so maybe you will listen.

You learned of your power
when you took
the Massachusetts woman
down. You locked
her out, ignored her
didn't invite
or broadcast
her opinion
until her fans dropped
away and her money dried
up.
It's an age-old tactic.
Just ignore
the outspoken woman,
put her
in your sound-proof cage

until she feels
she cannot breathe
charge her
with hysteria,
claim she is a radical
the worst ever
a heretic
a whore
maybe a Socialist
or a Communist, define
her as undependable

Name her Mary.
I will free
her sisters,
free the sisters
of Mary.

The levees hold
against deluge
there is much damage
some loss of life
the oil fields
are disrupted
scientists say the two
are linked. How
many hurricanes
will Louisiana endure?
How many
mildew-streaked
FEMA trailers
will house
the displaced
women with
six children
after years
have passed
and the big box
focuses on the
girls in tribal lands?
The oil money stains
the hearts
of lawmakers
soils the minds
of Gulf citizens fills
the coffers
of candidates
all in for the world's
warming.

The young
will have visions

the elderly's dreams
become crowded
with beloveds
the prolonged kisses
on bare skin
the snow
a frozen shower
slushy pearls
falling outside
a picture
window adds
to the sentiment
of a quiet place
in winter
to be in
on a day when
the private
was so real
it was unnoticeable
accessible
attainable
reserved
for investigative
journalists
living
for curiosity

and adventure.
Ideology
was present
and unmoving
Barry Goldwater types
with skinny ties
mostly shunned
loved by
the worst
of extremists.

You will surveil me
and not know where
my power comes from.

Her name was Julissa.
She was born
registered
as a welfare
baby reunited
to a known
abusive family.
She was seven years old
when found dead
beaten
a trauma

to the abdomen.
She was last
seen with a food voucher
waiting for a sandwich
at a vendor.
She crossed
a busiest city intersection
alone, everyone knew
she was alone
but did not interfere.
Her brother killed her
because she ate his snacks
for supper.

Name her
Mary, it is my greatest
hope to free the sisters
of Mary.

The time is here
when the weak prevail
they come out
of their hiding
their shelters
their backrooms
their caves
and stairwells

the lepers
with the affected limbs
are relocated
to an island
in paradise.
It has been said.
It has been written
Who am I
to doubt
the power
of language
of a higher will
aimed at
goodness
sweetness
and light?
It portends
the end
of hatred
of falsehood
of battles
of might
of hollow men
who torture
and kill
the vulnerable.

II

Write a poem about men
and some will rush
to the bookstore
or search
for it online.
They will want
to see if there
is flattery
any deserved glory
about obvious
heroics.
They want
to know
if the narrative
is about guns
about conquests
in exotic locales.
Write about women
and they expect
the same.
Women escape
notice
unless they
are in glossy
photographs
are young
or a toned 56
and can fit
into a leopard print
or are seen on
the arms
of sports figures.

Name her Mary. I want
to free the sisters of Mary.

The Catholic Church
is a brotherhood
a hierarchy
of robed men
who allow
women religious
to serve
to work
to labor
for parishes
while never letting
them set policy
or act as priests.
I suggest,

as one who loves
the Church,
that this is over. Lives
have been spent
fighting
the domination.
The woman
is considered
inferior
not by God
but by colleagues.
She is obedient
to tradition
and the biases
of old clergy.

Name her Mary, I am
called to free
the sisters of Mary.

Religion must
free its women
in cultures around
the world.
If in these, women
were equal

there would be
a sound
of freedom
so real
so joyous
so wonderful
so rapturous
so happy
that music
would play
bells would
tumble
and roll
sounding
in towers
until the moon
meets the morning sun.
Girls could settle
into community schools
there would
be no limits.

The storm moves
to Mississippi
up to New York.
The concern

is about heavy
rainfall.
Residents assess
the damage
to property
the fallen trees
the torn roofs.
Evacuees return home
anxious
and weary.
There are limitations
to words
to poetry
but the proclamation
is endless hope
is a promise
Christ's model
his example
from a mountaintop
where he called
for the Kingdom
It endures
and finds its way.

An open black book
with gold lettering
is set on a dictionary stand.
It contains
so many words
they signify
the potato peeler
the automobile
whirring machines
without emotion
every human sentiment
is felt most
when passionately
in love.
Once I put humiliation
into words
and am better
for it.

Great anger goes
into words
and there is no victory.
It is easy
to express.
It burns its way
onto paper
until all
is consumed

leaving nothing.
So be resolute
say the world
matters
is important
is worthwhile
even in
its current form
with troubles
and strife.
Say that after
the disappointment
of history people
will change
but they
will need
to read
four gospels
the social philosophers
the diaries
of part-time lunatics
and thinkers.
Whatever they read,
they will learn.

My words recognize

the price
the toll
the requirements
to go forward
in a time when
grace
leniency
mercy
seem over
and the law prevails
I remember the day
when I rushed
into the Sunday chapel
and knew.
I could see
the reversal.
The trials
would be real
the yoke
would be
placed
on shoulders
then bruising
then grooving
then sculpting
the flesh

the senses
of yesterday's holy
followers.

What I do today
will affect 20 years
from now
unworked legs
become soft;
shelved books
create stale minds.
Then there
are the read volumes
the Boston ad
and the ministry school.
It all comes back
perfectly
a messenger pigeon.

The present
catapults itself
into invisible hours
the birds
I see today
will have broken nests
straw gray
and dusty
with a bit
of a fisherman's string.
or clumps
of animal hair.
Time shows
me the past,
and I will know
the exact focus
of the future.

III

1. Frances Perkins
FDR's labor secretary
is a footnote
on a page
that says she
actually wrote
The New Deal
an important
economic plan.
President Roosevelt
took credit
for her brainpower
for helping
the suffering
millions
in breadlines.
How many times
does the man
take the glory
the recognition
for a woman's work?
How many times
does she collude
with mistreatment
cast her lot
with glamorous
well- constructed
Yahoo page
celebrities
who would
shape their bodies
with a surgeon's
knife?

2. Adrienne Rich
knew the potential
of poetry.
Words are
accountable.
How beautifully
you explain
what is in every
poet's mind before
she/he/ they
write the words
on the screen
The poetry frees
cowardly impulses
putting into
sentences
jarring witness.

You still teach
You did not die
but have "verbal privilege"
your words ran
fast through
my mind
I imagine
that I discovered
you, your command
of language
at a fateful time.

3. Margaret Fuller
   Hawthorne's muse,
   the model
   for Prynne
   became a shipwrecked
   mother
   of letters
   a journalist
   a war correspondent
   a Transcendentalist
   who is mostly
   forgotten
   removed
   from stories
   of Emerson
   of Thoreau
   the intellectuals
   who could
   not understand
   the desire
   to educate women.

4. Dorothy Day,
   a bohemian youth
   later a convert
   who worked
   tirelessly
   for the poor, who
   was vilified
   for entering
   the political realm
   and called
   the most radical
   candidate
   for sainthood,
   a Communist,
   and an anarchist.
   She was made
   a Servant of God
   and left on
   the Vatican's porch

IV

Holy Mary, pray for us.
Holy woman of God …
Holy woman of women

Woman … of Christ …
Woman … of divine grace …
Woman … most amiable …
Woman … most admirable …
Woman … of good counsel …
Woman … of our Creator …
Woman … of our Savior …

Woman … most prudent …
Woman … most venerable …
Woman … most renowned
Woman … most powerful …
Woman … most merciful …
Woman … most faithful …

Mirror of Justice …
Seat of Wisdom …
Cause of our joy …
Spiritual Vessel …
Vessel of Honor …
Singular Vessel

of Devotion ...
Mystical Rose ...
Tower of David ...
Tower of Ivory ...
House of Gold ...
Ark of the Covenant ...
Gate of Heaven ...
Morning Star ...
Health of the Sick ...
Refuge of Sinners ...
Comforter
of the Afflicted ...
Help of Christians ...

Woman ... of Angels ...
Woman ... of Prophets ...
Woman ... of Apostles ...
Woman ... of Martyrs ...
Woman ... of Confessors ...
Woman ... Conceived
without Original Sin ...
Woman ... Assumed
into Heaven ...
Woman ... of the Most Holy Rosary ...
Pray for us, O Holy Woman of God.

V

Finally, the open door
bright air
bricks fall
concrete exposes
broken
bent steel rods
that have kept her
so unheard.
She has been yelling
inside thick walls.
Now she steps out
amazed
at freedom
there is the unbelievable
the impossible
stacked straw
sweaty livestock
nature's mute feeling
inarticulate life
The outside knows her.
Her words
are faint at first
She reminds them
and they recall
the restraints, cut skin,
bruised bones
from trying to walk
on a straight path
She is through
the passage
her gait is steady
and shoes sound
one after another
She moves forward
without barricades
to be arriving
at anticipated places
the proclamation
the lifted voice
announces sings
about confinement's end

Painful fetters
of tradition
of old habits
are broken.
Let the woman
remember
what holds her
what keeps her

tied to salons
the all-color
discount
the French manicure
the dream
of baubles
of objects
of rooms
with the ultimate
tanning booth.
No, fill young minds
with equations
and musical
theories
for the piano
for symphonies
fill the young
with self-knowledge
with a passion
for unity.
Sit them
on wooden
stools
to study galaxies.
Let them count
the glittering stars

measure
the black holes
and make plans
to speak
to publish papers
on hurricanes
on the Earth
on climate change
let listeners
be of choice
who will hear
the sounds
in solar-powered
buildings
with open
windows
and welcoming
doors.

Atlantic disturbances
are reversing
wide rivers.
Harvard University
divests its endowments
from fossil
fuel companies

after alumni
protests.
The power goes out
in the sweltering
Southern cities
without AC.
Will young women
prophesy
while the old ones
dream dreams?
Perhaps they know
the sisters
are free, free
are the sisters of Mary.

At the Edge
of the Cities Burning

Preface

I am writing this preface near the third Sunday of Advent, which comes December 11 in 2022. Advent is a time of anticipation, a time when Catholic Church liturgy focuses on a second coming of Jesus Christ. I have become a woman who waits for the new kingdom. I can think of nothing more important to do than to hope for peace and a coming together of adversaries.

The Russian-Ukrainian War, the reality of climate change, both prompt uncertain times and cast shadows on daily life. In this small book, I explore the darker side of the early 21st Century's current events, as well as the glory of the Triune God, a God that was revealed to me when I audited the fall class, "The Mystery of the Trinity," at Boston College's School of Theology and Ministry.

Rafael Luciani, the brilliant Venezuelan theologian taught the online class, and his reflections were so deep that the only way I could find a sufficient response to them was through poetry. With verse, I became articulate.

Yet, let me be clear. *At the Edge of the Cities Burning* are my thoughts, with the concerns I have touched on throughout my writing career. It might shock some readers, even Christians to mention hell. Still, I am convinced that there are inherent sorry effects when we deny God's essence or ethics and do not promote the well-being of humanity and creation; people's souls are accountable. The world yearns for a humankind that knows there are consequences for actions.

Finally, readers might wonder if *At the Edge of the Cities Burning* is political or religious. It depends upon the lens in which the poem is read; the politico will see politics, while disciples will grasp its religious scope. The poem has been called both, "depressing" and "beautiful." Its effects are in the "eye of the beholder," which is why I consider it an important work for the era.

Mattie McClane, December 2022, Wilmington, NC

I

*"The Spirit of the Lord is upon me.
because he has anointed me
to bring glad tidings to the poor.
He has sent me to proclaim liberty
to the captives, and recovery of sight
to the blind and let the oppressed
go free and to proclaim a year
acceptable to the Lord."*

Rolling up the scroll, he handed it back to the attendant and sat down. All in the synagogue had their eyes fixed on him.

— *Luke 4:18-20*

I looked into
the eyes
of a working poet
and found
a peaceful soul
the calm
from saying
from witnessing
the world
as it is,
hard

but truthful
facts.

Later, an old lady
told me she
was taken
by the Holy Spirit
one day
while ironing. She
did not tell me
if it was a skirt

or blouse
that she straightened
only that her mind
and body
were filled
with joy. This,
while the world
was burning.
the orange fire of missiles
crowding
the tube's screen
this desert storm,
where men
would die.
Of course,
there were commercials
interruptions
from the faraway
unfelt pain. So
why is
the poet
calm and why
does
the elderly
woman tell me
of her bliss?

Tell me what
is to be done
when people
only love
slightly,
narrowly
their own? Humanity
might take
action, protest
the waste
the desolation
of souls. I am
a poet who
has loved much
and looked
on hell
felt the distress
the extreme discomfort
and prayed
to that chain-cutter
the God of wisdom
and freedom.

I am restless
with an ardent desire

of radiant light
seeing
its shadows
my fingers
type, and I know
that the forces
of good and harm
are palpable
It's no Sunday
preacher's dream
no dishonest
ploy for loose change
or greenbacks
to obtain power
each with followers
who both cry
for the word justice.

I recognize my privilege
my situation
my elite station,
and I wonder
if I can tell
this story.
I have watched
the hellish clock
the same time
that is kept
in nursing homes
and prisons.
The hands
change
slowly,
and one waits
throughout
seeming eternity
for one visitor
who looks sane
or who might
not yell
out at night
about thieves
and intruders
or who can
carry on
a friendly conversation.

For 25 years
I zeroed in on
the public realm
to see
if I could find

and tell
what
is hidden.
You'll have
to surmise
to guess
at the real motive
the true
beneficiaries
for most
official actions.
Here comes
the saying
that advises
one to ignore
offered plans
in favor
of what
people do.
Watch,
realizing folks
are incapable
of saving
themselves
in present time.
They wait

for history
the narration
the compass
that is too late
they are repentant
sorry for crimes
the tipping
point
of environmental
calamity
reported
by yesterday's
scientists
prophets
who are cold,
preserved
in their graves.

The prophets
are mediators
revealing
the divine
presence
of the unbegotten
who hears
the cries

of the poor
many stories
within the great one.
You will know
the vocation
when books
are banned. When
the gatekeepers
edit and erase
treatises
taking words out
of context
or simply

confiscating texts
on the way
to archives.
She/he/they
will be the target
of ridicule
of harassment
given the option
of obscurity
or death
while at
the edge of
the cities' burning.

II

*The people in the synagogue were
furious when they heard this. They got
up, drove him out of town, and took him
to the edge of the hill on which their city
was built, in order to throw him off the cliff.
But he walked right through the crowd and
went on his way.*

— Luke 4:28-30

The old woman
cleaned
the oak pews
after services
at a little
church known
as a wedding
venue in Iowa.
She told me
that she waited
for Jesus.
to come back
for a second time.
I was a young 30
dismissing
the statement
as a common
elderly wish.
After all, what
was she to look
forward to
at her age?
When she died,
they found
news clips in her Bible.

the fossil fuels
are burning
the forests
are burning
the vineyards
are burning

the oceans
are burning
the coral reefs
are burning
the mountains
are burning
the houses
are burning
the businesses
are burning
the corporations
are burning
the cities
are burning.

The aggressor says
America set
the precedent
for nuclear war
with Hiroshima
and Nagasaki.
When is military might
called just?
The powerful
make soldiers
of fathers
and sons
mothers
and daughters:
for what gain?
The borders
are expanded
as is the survivors'
hatred. The
political realm
is the search
the constant aim
for advantage
the upper hand
for how many members
are in legislatures
the consuming
high lifestyles
of wealthy white men.

I looked into the eyes
of a great
theologian
and found
a humble spirit.
He says God
wants people

to live in relationship
in community.
How radical
is the call
for the humanization
of people
who would be
not perfect
but more perfect
because of Christ.
The essence
of the Triune God
is wholeness
and unity,
the three are one.
God is the God
of time
before time.
God is the God
of history
before history
God is the God
of creation
before creation.
God is the God
of the poor
before the poor
God is the God of
language
before language.

God is the God of love
no beginning
and no end.

You'll not listen
to wise people
who seem
to know
how the world
should be.
The Spirit
put tongues
of flame above
the heads
of holy disciples
and in everyday
language
all language
followers spread
the lessons
of the poor

from the transcendent
the begotten
Word, the hope
for the reign
of the new kingdom.
The old order
will pass away.
Let it pass away.

III

The apartment
building's units
are left
without walls
like doll houses
in the nursery
the view
of homes
abandoned
torn, fluttering
insulation
broken drywall
once thoughtful decor
domestic
spaces open
to the wind.
Below,
the dogs circle
the warzone
they amble
through
the soot-layered grass
smoky skies
blue mornings
in search
of masters
missing
who have fled
with families
grandmothers
unsuspecting
children
with backpacks
carrying toys
all in a hurry
to escape
the missiles
the sirens
the explosions
with the instinct to live.

the coal
is burning.
the oil
is burning.
the Artic
is burning.
North
America
is burning.

Europe
is burning.
Africa
is burning.
Asia
is burning.
South
America
is burning.
Australia
is burning.
Antarctica
is burning.
continents
are burning.

I looked into
the eyes
of a public servant
and saw
a heart
and mind
recognizing
the potential
to connect
humankind.

Ballots
are testimonies,
the many voices
brought
to the table.
With popular
rule, there
are options
choices
for practical action
for compassion,
a tender
nurturing
feeling
for the planet
using
experiences
of place
of time
of history
to include
others
into a larger story.

Walt Whitman
thought

democracy
promotes
brotherhood.
Many folks
share a bond
through a
benevolent
government
system, where
each person
counts
and is afforded
God-given dignity.

Jane Addams
a social reformer,
wanted
democracy
to be more
than a vote
but a way
of living,
complete
social ethics
an appreciation
of knowledge
of diverse stories.

The essence
of the Triune God
is equality,
the three
are equal.
God is the God
of fairness
no beginning
and no end.
God is the God
of inclusion
no beginning
and no end
God is the God
of truth
no beginning
and no end.
God is the God
of justice
no beginning
and no end.
God is the God
of mercy
no beginning

and no end.
God is the God
of peace
no beginning
and no end
God is the God
of freedom
no beginning
and no end.

People begin
to journey
to walk
to escape war's
destruction,
uninhabitable
land. They
congregate
in border
towns
at outdoor
kitchens
with soup kettles
the luxury
of hot food

of charity.
They gather
near water
to wash dirty
clothes
the smell
of sweat
is everywhere
at only the start
of the world's
movement.

High temperatures
extreme
weather
kill the crops,
the rice
is burning
the wheat
is burning.
the corn
is burning.
the flax
is burning
the barley

is burning
the oats
are burning
the soybeans
are burning.
the vegetables
are burning.
the grasslands
are burning.

You'll not listen
to teachers
to farmers
to pastors
to thinkers
to scientists
who seem
to know how
the world
should be. You
will want
to deny
or adapt
to crisis.
Folks cannot
save themselves
in present time.
Families will
migrate
when fields
are dry
and crack
looking like puzzle
pieces.

I looked into
the eyes
of an ordinary
woman
and saw
every woman,
her second-rate status
her concerns
about oppression
and violence
at home
in the workplace
She is not free
or equal
in her own
relationships
and communities.

The aggressor's army
is pushed back
losing
territory.
Officials
discuss
using nuclear
weapons.
Will they sooner
or later?
With winter
coming,
they strike infrastructure
power sources.
The people prepare
to suffer
in the cold
and dark.
The cities
are burning.

The world
might become
a battlefield.

Tokyo
is burning.
Delhi
is burning.
Shanghai
is burning
Sao Paulo
is burning
Mexico City
is burning
Beijing
is burning.
Osaka
is burning.
New York
is burning.

IV

"I, John saw another angel come up from the East, holding the seal of the living God. He cried out in a loud voice to the four angels who were given power to damage the land and the sea. 'Do not damage the land, the sea or the trees until we put the seal on the heads of the servants of our God...' After this I had a vision of a great multitude which no one could count, from every nation, race, people, and tongue. They stood before the throne and the lamb... They cried out in a loud voice,
'Salvation comes from our God, who is seated on the throne and from the Lamb'"

– Rev. 7:2-4

I looked into the spirit
of a living God
and found
a companion
and a liberator
who frees humankind
from mistakes
who restores
shattered places
making new
a broken world.

The Tale of the Ancient Haberdasher

Preface

The Tale of the Ancient Haberdasher presents a 97-year old men's clothing chain owner whose story unfolds while being near death. I enter into the world of patriarchy, where fine menswear is hegemonic, representing society's dominant class with all its perks and privilege.

Ollie Anders has always believed in appearances: his stores' motto is "Appearance will Take You Far." Ollie believes his high-dollar clients are naturally good men because they appear so. He insulates himself from public happenings like war, violence, and famine, fostering his well-kept illusions. Until one day in a Zurich hotel he literally sees the light and is changed. Ollie begins to see the essences of men. He initially resists the demise of illusions, but is finally a new man.

The 20th Century philosopher Hannah Arendt believed that human essences are recovered in stories. I believe human essences are souls, which can be very different from our appearance.

While Ollie Anders' life is focused on the superficial, in the end, he is capable of deep remorse. He intends to tell the clergy his shortcomings.

Also, the reader will note that women are poor, marginalized, or unnamed in my poem, as in patriarchy. True, many women participate in a man's world with finesse and even success. Still I think they are actually exceptions, when one looks at at the worldwide status of women.

Mattie McClane, March 25, 2024

I

It is said life passes before
one's eyes
in the end
in pictures,
in images
in special memories
in realized dreams
of being
in a lover's arms
in crisis
in tragedies
forgotten
but drilled
into the psyche attached
for the weighty hold
keeping close
to the heart
all the hidden
is renewed
in space
displayed before
the king
the authority
without words

the signs
are baffling linguistics
and that's why
Ollie Anders called
the priest
one windy March day
because all
belief came
in front of him.
He saw his years
now 97
in full view
the moments
he'd forgotten
the narrative begins
the stories
the tale of
the ancient haberdasher
left in a physician's
porch garden
beside resting chairs
in lilies
and tulips
for it was spring

when the young mother
left him with a note:
"I am too poor
to care for my baby."
He squirmed
and cooed
like a dove
in the greenery
lush beds
smears
of earthworms
dirt colored
his bare cheeks
then a cleaning lady
found him
and brought
to the joyous
housewife
who was barren
at middle age.

Joy melds
with pity,
and she adopted
the infant
vowing

that he'd never
appear disadvantaged
to the world.
The baptismal gown
long and flowing
like a lake swan,
then every costume
under the sun
soldier suits
clown masks
judges' robes
cowboy chaps
a privileged child
he grew strong
and he was clever
so smart
he opened
his first men's
clothing store at 26,
the haberdasher
who would
open more outlets
in capital cities
become
the merchant
dressing senators

The Tale of the Ancient Haberdasher

every kind
of politician
came to him
for cashmere
overcoats
virgin wool jackets
to appear
their bests
to gain trust
to shake
an ordinary hand.
Ollie Anders
covered
very good men.

He imagined
his customers
his clients
and never wondered
about persona:
I was the I
seemingly authentic
worthy
and upright
as were
his intentions

his prayers
with visits
to the cathedral
first to marry
his bookkeeper
then on Sundays
evermore.

Sven, Peter,
and Rolf
were his sons
kept in respectable attire
from youth
reflecting
a successful father
who held
an illusion
of being self-made,
an heir
who had forgotten
his parents' love
and gift
of privilege. So
he dressed
the boys
for advancement.

He dreamed
they would be leaders
writing
interpreting laws.
They would
represent
their communities
with patterned
matching
shirts and ties. He
would take them
to the stores
to church
and the country club.

The raid began before dawn, with Israeli military's spokesman, a rear admiral, saying in a video statement that troops were operating in a "limited areas" of the hospital complex. More than twelve hours later, the enemy forces were engaged in fierce fighting near the hospital.

II

SVEN

His shirttail
was never tucked in,
Sven Anders
the oldest
seemed like
the one
who would learn
the men's clothing
business.
In the 1980s,
he dated
a few girls
and put his
father's clothes
in the cedar
closet and went
to New York
to become
an actor
winning a few
auditions
bit parts
and new friends
Ollie tried
to lure
him back
home
with offers
of management posts.
He could have
his own store: acting
was unstable
bohemian
with an
unpredictable
future
The father heard
stories
of late nights
with women
and men.
Ollie put on
a best suit
he was

going to rescue
his son.
He arrived in the city
in time to meet
with a doctor:
Sven was dying of AIDS.
He was dead at 32.

Experts project that Northern Gaza will face famine conditions as soon as next month, and half the enclave's population would suffer deadly levels of hunger, according to a new report from the global authority that has classified food security crises for decades.

The report released Monday projected that famine was "imminent" for 300,000 people where conditions would develop by the end of May. And by mid-July as many as 1.1 million people could face an "extreme lack of food, severe levels of starvation, death, destitution, and acute malnutrition.

III
PETER

Peter was accepted
to a top-tier
law school
in Massachusetts
graduated
with honors
a golden sash
and went on
to work
as a lobbyist
for a national
organization
that wrote laws
for state legislators.
Around dinner
and drinks
dry martinis
he pushed
several
thinktanks'
agendas
on environmental safety
on social programs
on the climate,
he was to cut
government
regulations
wherever they
could be found.
Peter's father
was no scholar
was no policy wonk
wasn't sure
what the son did,
but he was fitted
in-store
measured
for Ollie's best line
of suits. Naturally,
Ollie Anders
was proud,
very proud. So
respectable.

Trucks carrying lifesaving humanitarian relief for Gaza Strip were idle for days or weeks in Egypt waiting for inspectors to let them enter, and some were rejected despite having vital medical supplies. "The biggest solution is to open as many corridors as you can," said a state agency official.

IV

ROLF

The men's clothing
operation
the stores
in many
locations
fell to Rolf
the youngest son
who was on a plane
every week
checking
the brick
and mortar
status
of the father's
empire.

Rolf, a dandy
who delighted
in fine clothes
sporting
a perfectly
trimmed
beard
and manicured
nails. He
referred
affectionately
to his mother
as the bookkeeper,
as his father
did as well.
she was in fact
an accountant.

"Your Appearance
Can Take You Far"
was the company
motto
It went
along with a
silk brand
tag sewn
on custom suits.
Employees

were told
to shear
extra yards
of fabric
from the bales
the customer

wouldn't be the wiser.
The haberdasher's
lifelong
investment
pursuit was thriving.

The delegations' trip came after adversaries failed to reach an agreement ahead of the holy month. The delegation was led by the head of foreign intelligence and internal security services.

V

OLLIE

With his son
and wife
running
the business,
he found himself
traveling
to tradeshows.
At breakfasts,
he ate a toasted muffin
with jam.
He'd survey
venders' goods
of earth tone cloth
soft wools
dyed cashmere
the latest
blends
and synthetics.
He was a lucky man
His losses
were held at bay
by thinking
of the latest trends
in menswear.
Yet one day
while in a Zurich hotel
a light came into
his eyes
from the room's
wall-like windows.
It was an extraordinary
happening: the sun's
brilliant
rays seemed
to blind him
and he felt
somehow
he'd been changed,
but the experience
was fleeting.
He left the city.

Upon arriving home,
the nightly news

entered
his thoughts
more poignantly
he was now aware
of the great
violence,
the wars,
the chaos,
that he'd blocked
out. Surely,
it wasn't
new. It
was always
there. Why
hadn't he noticed?
As if a dream.
Ollie saw a group
of children
holding
out tin plates
asking for food
from an authority.

Now Ollie
remembered
his advanced years.

He was an old man.
He was a sick man.
His mind
was playing
tricks on him.
He thought
for a minute
he could see
men's souls
hear the cries
of the wounded.

The blue sky
looked dusty
with powder
clouds
thick
then thinning
in traces.
He remembered
William
Tecumseh
Sherman's
war coat,
how it survived
for several

decades
after his death
in an Atlanta
museum.
Was this
the legacy
of the haberdasher?
Were objects
rather than men
the story
of his life?
Were the seemingly
upstanding
often responsible
for much strife?

He no longer knew
what he understood.
He called
to the bookkeeper
to his wife
to Gretchen.
He felt bodily
sadness
deep physical
remorse
then emerging love.
Ollie rested
on his bed, waiting
for the priest.
He passed in his sleep.

Occupying Nazareth

I

It was a time
of would-be autocrats
bought lawmakers
and hesitant men
the only votes
that seemed
to count
or to matter
were for local offices
total tallies
for municipal
candidates
with the vision
to look ahead.
This was true
in Nazareth, Ohio
in the year 2030.
There was a party election
night
balloons
and confetti filled
the grand hall
the half-circular lobby
of a defunct paper
company
the smells of wet
pulp still rose
from the plastered
walls broken
in places
making unique designs.
The sturdy people gathered
the light of hope
in their eyes. Horace Bain
made promises
vowed
restaurants
would come back
after the jobs
and wages
would be
higher than ever before.
Industries
would be taxed
roads repaved.
They called it train town.
Now it was Horace
Bain's town

with the whistles
blowing out
warnings
to the younger set
see the elders'
unfulfilled dreams
the pool
that took what talent
there was
in a land
of little opportunity.

Bain presented
a plan
for renewal
advertised
the town online
in pamphlets
in classifieds
on the East Coast
on the West Coast
where extreme conditions
the mighty
hurricanes sent
rolling balls
of palm
fronds
and wildfires
grew in numbers.
"Come live
in train town
and put weather
worries down."
Citizens elected
him mayor.
Could he deliver
a mass migration?

Days after
the victory
gathering
he drove through
the city alone
to find
three rusty
and abandoned cranes
that looked
like a tall bunch
of blighted
bananas.
The parking lots
where buildings

once stood
went on
for miles
along the one-ways.
Horace had raised
expectations.
Suppose few
responded
to his invitation?
Suppose
he would be
a laughingstock
in his own hometown?
The prairie winds
were fierce
in April. Trees
swayed like dancers
hearing
a swift tempo.
All he could see
was defeat
yet imagining
victory
as his car
shimmied
jiggled

meeting bumps
on the asphalt
patchwork.
What would entice
others to relocate?
he'd sweeten the pot
offer $50,000
per family
to newcomers.

Horace Bain began
a PR campaign
to the town's residents:
"Clean Up Our Town."
mow lawns
trim bushes
and plant trees.
Still there
was a problem:
the homeless
were eyesores
congregating
near churches
and food pantries
in meandering lines
that could thwart

his best ideas
of rejuvenation.
He encouraged
residents
to buy one decent outfit
for video day
when crews
would highlight
the green growing grain
peach sunsets
well-dressed
children.
he would tour
the affluent
neighborhoods
where three-car
garages
were the norm.
By summer,
he was ready
the town
would put its
best footage forward.

In July, prospects
out of towners
began to inquire
about housing
and yearly rainfall
Westerners
wanted to know
if there were any
atmospheric rivers
or dry forests.
Carolinians
expressed relief
that there
were no
torrential rain
events
People were
interested.
People were coming
to where
hundreds
of small framed
houses
dotted the land.
Would these newcomers
be a monied class
be comfortable
in train town's culture?

Horace Bain
dismissed
the question.
locals
desperately
wanted renewal
and seldom
counted a cost.

II
THE MAYOR

Horace Morris Bain Jr.
followed
his father's
example
and worked
in the shops
just short
of 19.
Ginger
and freckled,
he was a welder whose
protective
apron
with its burnt
pinholes
looked
like stars
in the Milky Way.
he attached
the brakes
on automobiles
steel onto steel
year after year
until the plant
closed down.
Wide empty
storage
buildings
told the story
of workers
with nowhere to go.
Horace took
a class to be
a financial planner.
he worked
at the bank
as a teller
as a loan officer
as a vice president
then ran
for alderman
in the 3rd district
His career
and passions
was beginning
to emerge.

No one would
have guessed
he'd one day be mayor
of the ailing,
rusting,
community.
He had cleaned up
the town
except
for the bleakness
of the wanderers
the homeless
who'd make
their trek
every morning
from the shelter
near the convent
and old fire station:
to the coolness
of the library
on summer
afternoons.

At the convent's door
a heavy
walnut slab
of an entrance
the mayor pleaded
with Sister Frances
to keep
the unfortunates off
the streets
the sidewalks
out of the sight
of coastal visitors.
He explained
the large sum
of money
involved
for each newcomer.
The nun asked,
"Why give
to the newcomer
while some
here are still
suffering?"
He was silent.
He begged
for cooperation.
In his mind,
he answered
her question:

money given
to the poor
never increased.
It was a bad
investment.
He had made promises.
It wasn't cruelty.
It was sound business.

Fall's festivities
filled the calendar
cold beer
hot bratwurst
polka dances
people
were happy
trees turned
to the deep
colors of autumn
maroons
golds
grocery prices
seemed lower.
everyone
was abuzz
with anticipation
of signed contracts
the newcomers
would arrive soon,
early next spring.
This winter
was a time
of preparation,
the hours
to get ready. Train
town stood
to gain a future.

III
THE MEETING

The mayor called
December's
council meeting
to order.
Visitors
monied men
said they would
build a wind
turbine plant
if the community
could sustain it.
Dressed lightly
in the midwestern
winter chill,
the below zero
temperature
was more than
the business barons
imagined:
they shivered
when they talked.
Local developers
divided
the farmland
into building sites.
A speculator rose
and suggested
that old
smaller houses
be condemned
quickly razed
to make room
for construction.
newcomers
would need
better housing.

The time came
on the agenda
for citizen's input.
Sister Frances asked
for funding
for 20 new beds
at the homeless shelter.
The honorable mayor
was mortified:

Occupying Nazareth • 341

he confronted
the sister
after the meeting.
what was she trying
to do, scuttle
train town's
success? He
had told her
about keeping
the homeless problem
under wraps.
He could not
save them
surely, she agreed.
The sister replied,
"One cannot save
who are unacknowledged.
Won't you
look at them?"
Horace wanted
to tell her
that he saw them
at the grocery store
on the downtown streets
in his dreams.
He could not expect

her, who probably took
a vow of poverty
to understand
his plans
to resurrect train town.

Sister Frances came
close to him
in his space
and gently touched
his forearm. "If you
see them,
then their stories
their lives
and circumstances
would be real,
and you would act."
She told him
there would
be winners
and losers with
any remade
community.

Horace bet
on more winners

than losers
He now read reports
on extreme weather
on homeowner's
insurance
how many coastal
policies
were cancelled
after floods
and wildfires.
weary people
fleeing
to relocate
to the central
states
were his hope.
train town
boasted four
mild seasons
few natural disasters.

The sister seemed
to suggest
that the poor
would be
the losers: the
town was poor
after decades
of industries'
abandonment.
Horace not once
imagined
it could go down
further.

IV
SISTER FRANCES

When the Sisters
of St. Gregory
left town
because people
gave slim offerings
to the Church,
Sr. Frances stayed
behind
to care
for the very poor.
She kept
on her table
a stand-up cross
of Jesus
a warm crust
of bread
and a teacup.
She remembered
the town's
collections' plates
once filled
once heaping
the town bustling
with stores
and eateries.
After the auto plants left,
hucksters came in
there was talk
sham proposals
of the biggest
grandest
theme parks
sports arenas
flashy casinos
to light up
the now dark nights.
Horace was not
the first
to imagine
a restored city:
the others failed.

People were behind
Horace though.
While she
had doubts,

he promised
the clergy would
return, people
would build
new churches
and citizens
would renew
their faith
when they
had a better life.
Horace was a man
with attractive dreams.

In early spring
earthmovers
and demolition
crews began
to appear,
razing small
unpainted
already broken
houses
with displaced
daffodil
now atop
of dirt mounds
of debris like
a conqueror's flag.
For better
or worse,
progress
was everywhere
new buildings
to replace
the old.
Not common homes
but the best
that money
could buy.
People watched
as train town
became
a boom town.
The newcomers
began arriving
moving vans
pulled up
trailers
packed
with belongings
aluminum grills
deck chairs

colorful
sun umbrellas
the train towners
were gleeful
for what looked
so positive.
The new folks
seemed
fashionable
designer
clothing
print
dresses
and leather bags
upscale neighbors.

The privileged
migrants
overtook
overwhelmed
the locals
the disparity
between
the well-off
and the poor

grew. "Train
towners"
became a slur
for the sorry
and downtrodden:
the homeless
numbers
increased
but they
were invisible.
they were not seen
and rarely
spoken of.
The convent
was eventually
torn down.
Sister Frances
moved away,
returning
to the motherhouse
in Akron
where Jesus's
statue
was adored
and glorified.

Horace Bain lost
his bid
for reelection
to a newcomer
a hero
heart was crushed
the light
escaped from
familiar eyes
and he would hear
in his mind
until his dying day:
"Train Town
was Horace
Bain's town
with its whistles
blowing out
warning
to the younger set
see the elders'
unfulfilled dreams
the pool
that took
what talent
there was
in a land
of little opportunity."
Horace fulfilled
his promises.
How odd
it did not go
as he planned.

About The Author

Mattie McClane (Kristine A. Kaiser) is an American novelist, poet, and journalist. She is the second and youngest daughter born to James L. and Shirlie I. Myers in Moline, Illinois. Her father was a commercial artist and her mother worked as a secretary.

McClane's earliest education was in the Catholic schools. Her experience with their teachings deeply affected her. At a young age, she became aware of gender inequality. She credits her early religious instruction for making her think about "all kinds of truths" and ethical matters.

McClane's parents divorced when she was eight years old. Her mother remarried attorney John G. Ames and the new couple moved to a house beside the Rock River. The river centrally figures in McClane's creative imagination. She describes her childhood as being "extraordinarily free and close to nature."

McClane moved to Colorado and married John Kaiser in 1979, in Aurora, just East of Denver.

They then moved to Bettendorf, Iowa where they had three children. John worked as a chemist. Mattie became interested in politics, joining the local League of Women Voters. According to McClane, she spent her 20s "caring for her young children and working for good government."

She graduated from Augustana College with a B.A. degree in the Humanities. She began writing a political column for Quad-Cities Online and Small Newspaper Group, based in Illinois.

Her family moved to Louisville, Kentucky where she continued with her journalism and then earned an M.A. in English from the University of Louisville. Critically acclaimed author Sena Jeter Naslund directed her first creative thesis, "Unbuttoning Light and Other Stories," which was later published in a collection.

She was accepted to the University of North Carolina at Wilmington's M.F.A. in Creative Writing Program, where she wrote the short novel

Night Ship, working under the tutelage of Pulitzer Prize winning author Alison Lurie. McClane studied with Dennis Sampson in poetry also. She graduated in 1999.

She would write a column for the High Point Enterprise in North Carolina. She would later write for the News and Observer. McClane has regularly published commentary for over 25 years.

Mattie McClane is the author of

> *Night Ship: A Voyage of Discovery* (2003)
>
> *River Hymn: Essays Evangelical and Political* (2004)
>
> *Wen Wilson* (2009),
>
> *Unbuttoning Light: The Collected Short Stories of Mattie McClane* (2012)
>
> *Now Time* (2013)
>
> *Stations of the Cross* (2016)
>
> *The Mother Word: An Exploration of the Visual* (2017)
>
> *Simeon's Canticle* (2018)
>
> *The Song of the Grackle* (2019)
>
> *The Magnificent Light of Morning* (2021)
>
> *To Free the Sisters of Mary* (2022)
>
> *At the Edge of the Cities Burning* (2023)
>
> *The Tale of the Ancient Haberdasher* (2024)
>
> *Occupying Nazareth* (2025).

www.ingramcontent.com/pod-product-compliance
Lightning Source LLC
Chambersburg PA
CBHW071803080526
44589CB00012B/663